NEW
CREATION
MEDITATIONS

30 Days to the YOU
That's Already NEW

JOEL SIEGEL

New Creation Meditations ©2013 Big God Media

DEDICATION

This book is dedicated to the *precious fruit of the earth (James 5:7)* – multitudes who are coming to Christ as God's power sweeps the earth. They are asking, "Where do I find those verses?" Here is a portion of that which they seek, that they might know they are no longer the person they once were, but are a new species, a new race – a new creation.

CONTENTS

INTRODUCTION

New Creation Meditations is a 30-day action plan, designed to give believers at all stages of spiritual development a supply of spirit-food for quick growth. The lessons are filled with scriptures, and it is these scriptures that are the most valuable part of the book.

When athletes and body builders want to exceed the natural limitations of their bodies, they often turn to growth hormones to enhance their efforts. I like to think of the collection of verses in these lessons as *spiritual steroids* that will help take you beyond life in the natural. These growth supplements do have side effects such as increased spiritual awareness, enhanced levels of peace and joy, and a strong sense of dominion over the powers of darkness. Go ahead and load up!

As you read each day, you will discover a different aspect of our inheritance in Christ. Pay particular attention to the verses themselves; they have the power to transform your life. Although the lessons are arranged in a 30-day format, the truths that are presented within must be meditated upon throughout the course of your life. Keep this book handy for easy reference to these powerful scriptures. Read them carefully and refer to them often, keeping them in your heart and mouth always.

My son, be attentive to my words;
incline your ear to my sayings.
Let them not escape from your sight;
keep them within your heart.
For they are life to those who find them,
and healing to all their flesh.
Proverbs 4:20-22

MADE RIGHTEOUS

For our sake he made him to be sin who knew no sin, so that in him we might become the righteousness of God. 2 Corinthians 5:21

Most people, at some point, experience feelings of unworthiness or inferiority before God. Indeed, many believers spend their entire Christian lives living like outsiders. They may have knowledge that they are forgiven, but often do not know that something much greater than forgiveness has taken place. The believer has actually been made righteous.

*For as by the one man's disobedience the many were made sinners, so **by the one man's obedience the many will be made righteous**. Romans 5:19*

Think about the first man, Adam. Adam was made in God's image and likeness, and had no inhibitions about being in God's presence. In fact, the glory of God is where he felt most at home. To keep man safe, God commanded Adam and Eve to stay away from the tree that would bring spiritual death to the one who ate from it. They disobeyed, ate of the tree, and died spiritually, just as God had warned. Everything changed for God's man that day.

For the wages of sin is death, but the free gift of God is eternal life in Christ Jesus our Lord. Romans 6:23

The aprons they made from fig leaves to cover themselves couldn't fix their sin problem, and the blood of innocent animals only temporarily covered their sin. For the rest of their lives, Adam and Eve dealt with feelings of unworthiness and inferiority and, until Christ came, so did every other person on earth. Now, thank God, we are in the New Covenant, where we find the phrase "the righteousness of God" used to describe man.

1

*For I am not ashamed of the gospel, for it is the power of God for salvation to everyone who believes, to the Jew first and also to the Greek. For in it **the righteousness of God** is revealed from faith for faith, as it is written, "The righteous shall live by faith." Romans 1:16-17*

We have been made righteous with His righteousness. Our sins are not just forgiven, they are remitted – erased or rolled back as if they had never happened. We truly get a fresh start. When a person receives Christ as Lord, his or her spiritual condition is changed; the old sin nature is destroyed, and the spirit is recreated in the image and likeness of God. Paul describes this miraculous transformation in one of his letters to the church at Corinth:

*Therefore, if anyone is in Christ, **he is a new creation**. The old has passed away; behold, the new has come. 2 Corinthians 5:17*

The Amplified Bible says "he is a new creation altogether." I like that! That means we're no longer on the outside looking in. There's no reason to be distanced from God. God, through Christ, came down to our level so He could bring us up to His level.

It was to show his righteousness at the present time, so that he might be just and the justifier of the one who has faith in Jesus. Romans 3:24

Because we have been justified, or made righteous, God sees no difference between Jesus and us. We are no less righteous than He Himself is. That can be hard to believe for the person walking by sight – looking at his own performance or past – but we simply believe the declaration of the Bible and enjoy the benefit that comes as a result of what Christ has accomplished on our behalf.

*Little children, let no one deceive you. Whoever practices righteousness **is righteous, as he is righteous**. 1 John 3:7*

No, we don't deserve it. We never could earn this new condition of heart and position before God. It is a gift that we simply receive and walk worthy of. By His amazing grace we receive our righteous place, attentive to the righteousness that has been given to us.

*For if because of one man's trespass (lapse, offense) death reigned through that one, **much more surely** will those who receive [God's] overflowing grace (unmerited favor) and the free gift of righteousness [putting them into right standing with Himself] **reign as kings in life** through the one Man Jesus Christ (the Messiah, the Anointed One). Romans 5:17 (AMP)*

The Apostle Paul was as good as anyone at keeping the Old Testament law. But because his best efforts fell short, he was happy to throw away every bit of his past in order to know Christ and gain the righteousness that comes from Him.

*But whatever gain I had, I counted as loss for the sake of Christ. Indeed, I count everything as loss because of the surpassing worth of knowing Christ Jesus my Lord. For his sake I have suffered the loss of all things and count them as rubbish, in order that I may gain Christ and be found in him, not having a righteousness of my own that comes from the law, but that which comes through faith in Christ, **the righteousness from God** that depends on faith – that I may know him and the power of his resurrection, and may share his sufferings, becoming like him in his death. Philippians 3:7-10*

Never again think of yourself as a sinner. No longer think of yourself as only forgiven. You have been made righteous – every bit as righteous as He is. Walk in the light of the righteousness you have received and reign in life today.

Boldly make this confession:

> **I am a new creature. I have been made righteous. I am the righteousness of God in Christ. The old is gone, the new has come. I am righteous as He is righteous.**

DAY 2

FREE FROM SIN AND CONDEMNATION

Stand fast therefore in the liberty by which Christ has made us free, and do not be entangled again with a yoke of bondage.
Galatians 5:1 (NKJV)

If a Christian is living in sin, it's no one's fault but his own. That person needs to face that truth and take immediate action to stop the sin. He should look to God for the help He's made available through the Bible, His Spirit, even through his pastor and church family, understanding that sin is a choice. God redeemed us from sin's power by sending Jesus. Now, we must make the choice to take action against the desires of the flesh.

And those who belong to Christ Jesus have crucified the flesh with its passions and desires. Galatians 5:24

Too many Christians believe the lie that we can't help but sin with great regularity. I've actually heard people who were supposed to be believers comment that they sin so many times each day they couldn't possibly confess all their sins. What does the word say about that?

*No one born of God makes a practice of sinning, for God's seed abides in him, and **he cannot keep on sinning** because he has been born of God. 1 John 3:9*

If it's true that we all sin with great frequency, then Jesus' precious blood did not do its job of providing us with the power we need. No, let's just believe what the Bible says about this subject. Scripture teaches us that we are cleansed and removed far from sin as we walk in the light of God's Word, partaking of the things of God.

But if we walk in the light, as he is in the light, we have fellowship with one another, and the blood of Jesus his Son cleanses us from all sin. 1 John 1:7

4

Not only is it possible, it is fully expected that the believer will grow strong enough in spirit to live in a place of continual victory over sin and the flesh. Paul clearly stated the wonderful truth of sin's defeat.

*For **sin shall not be master over you**, for you are not under law but under grace. Romans 6:14 (NASB)*

The Message translation of this passage has great impact:

You must not give sin a vote in the way you conduct your lives. Don't give it the time of day. *Don't even run little errands that are connected with that old way of life. Throw yourselves wholeheartedly and full-time—remember, you've been raised from the dead!—into God's way of doing things.* ***Sin can't tell you how to live.*** *After all, you're not living under that old tyranny any longer. You're living in the freedom of God. Romans 6:12-14*

Sin should have no vote or voice in our lives. However, the believer who has not yet grown in grace and knowledge will continue to yield to the desires of the flesh and mind, and sin will result. In those cases, that person should immediately take action by turning from the sin, confessing it to the Lord, and receiving forgiveness and cleansing, by faith.

If we confess our sins, he is faithful and just to forgive us our sins and to cleanse us from all unrighteousness. 1 John 1:9

When Christians confess their sins, they often have trouble believing that they are cleansed and restored. That's because they still feel guilty. Those feelings of guilt are what the scriptures refer to as condemnation. Condemnation does not come from God, but from our own spirits, as our heart voices its disappointment for the decision to go astray. The mind and feelings pick up the condemnation and will hold on to it for as long as they are allowed.

*There is therefore **now no condemnation** to those who are in Christ Jesus, who do not walk according to the flesh, but according to the Spirit. For the law of the Spirit of life in Christ Jesus has made me free from the law of sin and death. Romans 8:1-2 (NKJV)*

We are free from sin, and there is no condemnation for us. If you've confessed and repented, you must believe that God has cleansed you just as He said. Refuse to believe any lingering feelings or emotions, and do not accept guilt or condemnation for it will rob you of the faith and confidence you need to receive from God.

Beloved, if our heart does not condemn us, we have confidence before God; and whatever we ask we receive from him, because we keep his commandments and do what pleases him. 1 John 3:21-22

Sin's power in your life has been broken. Condemnation can't stay. We are now living by the law of the Spirit of life in Christ, having been set free from the law of sin and death.

*We know that our old self was crucified with him in order that the body of sin might be brought to nothing, so that we would no longer be enslaved to sin. For one who has died has been **set free from sin**. Romans 6:6-7*

Your old sin nature is gone – dead. You are a new creature with power over sin. Walk in that freedom today.

Confession:

Sin is not my master. It has no power and no dominion over me. Sin has no say and no vote. The law of the Spirit of life has made me free from the law of sin and death.
I am free from condemnation. I have no negative history and no past because of Jesus' blood's cleansing power.

AUTHORIZED

*Behold, I have given you authority to tread on serpents and scorpions, and over **all** the power of the enemy, and nothing shall hurt you. Luke 10:19*

Our authority over the enemy's power in our lives is absolute – we have *all* authority over the devil in our lives. We cannot always exercise that same degree of authority over the enemy in the lives of other people we know, but we can in our own lives. If anything is to be done about the devil in our lives, we must do it. If this sounds repetitious, it's because this truth requires multiple hearings. It's so easy to wrongly believe that God will take care of the devil's activity where our lives are concerned.

*Truly, I say to you, whatever **you** bind on earth shall be bound in heaven, and whatever **you** loose on earth shall be loosed in heaven. Again I say to you, if two of **you** agree on earth about anything they ask, it will be done for them by my Father in heaven. Matthew 18:18-19*

Notice that someone must take action on earth before heaven steps in. If we will do something on earth, heaven will back us up. If we do nothing, heaven does nothing. Several other scriptures harmonize with this thought.

Submit yourselves therefore to God. Resist the devil, and he will flee from you. James 4:7

Who does the submitting to God? We do. Who resists the enemy? We do. It should be pointed out here that there is more than one side to this subject of authority. Authority doesn't just involve ruling over people or things, it also includes taking our place in submission at times. If a person doesn't learn to submit, he will never be successful in a place of authority. If we want to successfully use our authority over the devil, then we must first submit to God.

7

Be sober-minded; be watchful. Your adversary the devil prowls around like a roaring lion, seeking someone to devour. **Resist him, firm in your faith,** *knowing that the same kinds of suffering are being experienced by your brotherhood throughout the world. 1 Peter 5:8-9*

Again, it's our job to resist the devil, not God's job. We can truthfully say that God has already done all He's going to do about the devil until He slaps a chain around him and throws him into the pit. Until that day, Satan is seeking to devour, steal, kill, and destroy those who will let him. It's our job to **enforce his defeat** by taking our place of authority.

And give no opportunity to the devil. Ephesians 4:27

Notice that Satan evidently needs an open door, or opportunity, if he is to have access to our lives. If we're the ones who can open the door to let him in, we are also the ones who can keep the door shut, preventing him from having access. It is possible to keep the devil waiting on the outside indefinitely as we remain in obedience to God and are vigilant in our place of authority. Keeping the door shut to the enemy involves more than avoiding sin; it also requires regular attention to the things of God, staying alert and in our place.

Finally, be strong in the Lord and in the strength of his might. Put on the whole armor of God, that you may be able to stand against the schemes of the devil. For we do not wrestle against flesh and blood, but against the rulers, against the authorities, against the cosmic powers over this present darkness, against the spiritual forces of evil in the heavenly places. Therefore take up the whole armor of God, that you may be able to withstand in the evil day, and having done all, to stand firm. Stand therefore, having fastened on the belt of truth, and having put on the breastplate of righteousness, and, as shoes for your feet, having put on the readiness given by the gospel of peace. In all circumstances take up the shield of faith, with which you can extinguish all the flaming darts of the evil one; and take the helmet of salvation, and the sword of the Spirit, which is the word of God. Ephesians 6:10-17

There's no attack of the enemy that can prevail in my life if I will take my place of authority. Jesus, before He left earth, emphasized this truth to His disciples.

And these signs will accompany those who believe: in my name they will cast out demons; they will speak in new tongues; they will pick up serpents with their hands; and if they drink any deadly poison, it will not hurt them; they will lay their hands on the sick, and they will recover. So then the Lord Jesus, after he had spoken to them, was taken up into heaven and sat down at the right hand of God. And they went out and preached everywhere, while the Lord worked with them and confirmed the message by accompanying signs. Mark 16:17-20

We see a pattern in all these verses whereby we as believers and residents of earth exercise the authority God has given us, and then heaven's power backs us up. Thank God that He does, for what good is our authority if it's not reinforced by His power? We must boldly take the place of dominion that has been given to us by God.

*For if, because of one man's trespass, death reigned through that one man, much more will those who receive the abundance of grace and the free gift of righteousness **reign in life** through the one man Jesus Christ.* Romans 5:17

The Amplified translation of this verse says that we "reign in life as kings." Kings have supreme authority over their domain and they exercise it most often by simply issuing a command from the comfort of their throne. When they command, things go into motion. Likewise, when we speak words of faith – resisting, binding, loosing, etc, things begin to happen in the spirit-realm that bring heaven's power alongside our authority, causing great change to take place.

Confession:

> *I have authority over all the power of the enemy in my life. I rule and reign in my domain. When I resist the devil, he flees from me. He's terrified of me. He's afraid of me.*
> *As I speak in agreement with the word, heaven's power backs me up.*

IN HIM

For in him we live and move and have our being. Acts 17:28

One cannot read through the letters in the New Testament without encountering phrases such as *in Him*, *in whom*, and *in Christ* over and over. We should give extra attention to the verses where these phrases appear; they let us know who we are, what we have, and what we can do now that we have been born again. From God's viewpoint, these are statements of absolute fact irrespective of our human abilities, talents, faults, and failures. These verses are not to be doubted or argued, only believed, spoken, and acted upon. Paul spoke the most well-known and often quoted of these verses in the book of Philippians.

*I can do all things **through him** who strengthens me. Philippians 4:13*

What makes this a statement of fact rather than an outright lie? Two very important words: *through Him*. We know that without Him we can do nothing (John 15:5), but the two words *through Him* turn nothing into everything.

We've all seen movies or television shows where people are gathered around a gambling table, watching the players play. As the stakes get higher, the dealer may ask a player, "are you in?" If he is, he remains seated at the table and is subject to the rules of the game. I want you to know that if you are born-again, *you're in*. You're in Christ, a part of His body, part of God's family. You're a partaker of the benefits that come from being at His table, but you also have responsibilities that go along with being *in Him*.

*For we are his workmanship, created **in Christ Jesus for good works**, which God prepared beforehand, that we should walk in them. Ephesians 2:10*

Do you remember what life was like before you were in Christ, when you were only *in you*? We find, in this same chapter in Ephesians, a stark reminder of just how bad things were:

*At that time you were **without Christ**, being aliens from the commonwealth of Israel and strangers from the covenants of promise, **having no hope** and without God in the world. Ephesians 2:12 (NKJV)*

We were all hopeless cases, but thank God for the next verse:

*But now **in Christ** Jesus you who once were far off have been brought near by the blood of Christ. Ephesians 2:13 (NKJV)*

The first few chapters of the book of Ephesians are full of these great *in Him* statements that teach us about ourselves – the new creation. Notice just a few of them:

*He chose us **in him** before the foundation of the world. Ephesians 1:4*

***In whom** we have redemption through His blood. Ephesians 1:7*

***In him** we have obtained an inheritance. Ephesians 1:11*

***In him** you... were sealed with the promised Holy Spirit. Ephesians 1:13*

*For **through him** we both have access in one Spirit to the Father. Ephesians 2:18*

The following verse beautifully sums up what it means to be in Him.

*So then you are no longer strangers and aliens, but you are **fellow citizens with the saints and members of the household of God**. Ephesians 2:19*

Saying that we are fellow citizens with the saints and members of the household of God is another way of saying we're *in Him*.

It is very important to understand that God doesn't begin to see us in Christ when we receive Jesus; He has always seen us in Him (review

Ephesians 1:4.) It wasn't a reality in our lives until our personal enlightenment and conversion, but God has always seen the body of Christ as a whole unit, complete with all its members, past, present, and future. That means that when Jesus was on the cross, so were you. When He descended, you did too. When He was quickened, you were quickened. His raising was your raising, and His ascension and seating is also yours. Does God's Word agree with this? Absolutely!

*I have been **crucified with Christ**. It is no longer I who live, but Christ who lives in me. And the life I now live in the flesh I live by faith in the Son of God, who loved me and gave himself for me. Galatians 2:20*

*We were **buried therefore with him** by baptism into death, in order that, just as Christ was raised from the dead by the glory of the Father, we too might walk in newness of life. Romans 6:4*

*But God, being rich in mercy, because of the great love with which he loved us, even when we were dead in our trespasses, **made us alive together with Christ**— by grace you have been saved— and **raised us up with him** and **seated us with him** in the heavenly places in Christ Jesus. Ephesians 2:4-6*

To say we're in Christ is to state a profound truth. We must meditate on these spiritual truths until we see ourselves in the pages of the Bible, at the cross, in the resurrection, and at the ascension. We're not to see ourselves there *instead* of Jesus. He was our substitute – but we see ourselves as God sees us: with Jesus and in Him.

Confess this:

> *I am in Christ. I have been crucified with Him, and buried with Him. I have also been made alive with Him. I've been raised up together with Him, and I am seated with Him in heavenly places. Through Christ I can do all things. I am part of His family.*

CALLED UP

*That the God of our Lord Jesus Christ, the Father of glory, may give you a spirit of wisdom and of revelation in the knowledge of him, having the eyes of your hearts enlightened, that you may know what is **the hope to which he has called you**, what are the riches of his glorious inheritance in the saints. Ephesians 1:17-18*

These verses are part of a prayer that Paul was praying for believers in Ephesus. It is quite possibly the greatest prayer you or I could ever pray for other believers, especially for those going through difficulties, because failure in a Christian's life is not a result of what he doesn't have, but a result of what he doesn't know. If a Christian will *know* differently, he will *have* differently. What did Paul want these saints to know? He wanted them to know about the place to which they had been called.

We often read verses about our calling and begin to think about God's plan for our individual lives. Thank God for the plans He has for each of us individually, but these verses are emphasizing a common call – something that is part of the inheritance of every believer. Every Christian is called to take his or her place with Him, at the right hand of God.

The word *calling*, found a handful of times in the New Testament, means *an invitation*. Notice how this invitation is described in some other verses:

*I press toward the mark for the prize of **the high calling** of God in Christ Jesus. Philippians 3:14 (KJV)*

*Who saved us and called us to **a holy calling**, not because of our works but because of his own purpose and grace, which he gave us in Christ Jesus before the ages began. 2 Timothy 1:9*

*Therefore, holy brothers, you who share in **a heavenly calling**, consider Jesus, the apostle and high priest of our confession. Hebrews 3:1*

Our calling, or invitation, is high, holy, and heavenly, not earthly. It's a call to come up to where He is. Remember, we've been seated with Him in heavenly places (Ephesians 2:6.) We are invited to take the same high place He now occupies.

The glory that you have given me I have given to them, that they may be one even as we are one. John 17:22

Because one definition of the word *glory* is *an exalted state or position*, we could read this verse this way: *The exalted position you have given to me, I have given to them.* How exciting! This position is already ours, but we must have a revelation of that place, walking in the light of it.

Everything changes when we come up to our place. Our problems look smaller from our exalted position in Christ. This place belongs to us right now. We don't have to wait until we die and go to heaven to take our seat with Him. Even while on earth, the believer belongs to the heavenly world more than he or she belongs to this earthly one.

*But **our citizenship is in heaven**, and from it we await a Savior, the Lord Jesus Christ. Philippians 3:20*

Heaven is the home base from which we operate here on earth. The New Testament writers talked about how they considered themselves nothing more than strangers and pilgrims here on earth (Hebrews 11:13, 1 Peter 2:11). The place we are most at home is in our seat in heavenly places in Christ.

To truly see more of what our exalted position is like, look carefully at the remaining verses in Ephesians chapter one:

*And what is the immeasurable greatness of his power toward us who believe, according to the working of his great might that he worked in Christ when he raised him from the dead and seated him at his right hand in the heavenly places, **far above all rule and authority and*** *power and dominion, and above every name that is named, not only in this age but also in the one to come. And he put **all things under his feet** and gave him as head over all things to the church, which is his body, the fullness of him who fills all in all. Ephesians 1:19-23*

Because we're in Him, what is true about Him in these verses is also true about us. We have the kind of power that exceeds all other power available to us. We are seated with Him, far above all other authority, power, or names. As we look down from our place, we notice all our enemies are under our feet. Christ is the head, and we're the body, seated with Him in our exalted position.

After Paul prayed for the believers to see and know their place, he exhorted them not to neglect it, but rather to occupy it in a worthy manner.

I therefore, a prisoner for the Lord, urge you to walk in a manner worthy of the calling (place) *to which you have been called. Ephesians 4:1*

When a believer is always talking about how bad things are in life, we know they need to be reminded of where they are seated. There is no better view in life than the view from our exalted position in Christ. A long-running game show on television may have popularized the phrase "Come on down," but the believer has a different invitation awaiting him: "Come on up!"

Confession:

> *The eyes of my heart are enlightened. Therefore, I see and know the place to which He's called me. I've been given a rich, glorious, exalted place with Him. The same place Jesus has, far above every enemy. The devil is under my feet. I have a high, holy, and heavenly calling. I am walking worthy of this place to which I am called.*

RUN YOUR RACE, FINISH YOUR COURSE

*Therefore, since we are surrounded by so great a cloud of witnesses, let us also lay aside every weight, and sin which clings so closely, and let us run with endurance **the race that is set before us**, looking to Jesus, the founder and perfecter of our faith, who for the joy that was set before him endured the cross, despising the shame, and is seated at the right hand of the throne of God. Hebrews 12:1-2*

It should be foremost in our minds that we are on this planet for a purpose – taking our place in a divinely ordained plan, referred to in this scripture as our race. This race is also sometimes called the will of God for our lives. The Bible lays out His plans for us in a general sense, but there are also many details that must be discovered individually – those plans of His that apply just to you.

For I know the plans I have for you, declares the LORD, plans to prosper you and not to harm you, plans to give you hope and a future. Jeremiah 29:11 (NIV)

No one is born with a printout of all the details of God's plan for his or her life. Even Jesus had to discover the Father's plan for His life, then run every leg of His race with endurance in order to finish strong. No two people will ever have *exactly* the same race to run, so we must resist the temptation to copy someone else's course. Doing so would lead to failure, because the highest degree of success a person could ever attain is to run and complete *his or her* race, not another person's. Yes, be encouraged and inspired by the success of others, but don't adopt their race as your own. Doing so displays ignorance concerning the will of God. You only have grace for *your* race!

*But they are only **comparing themselves with each other, using themselves as the standard of measurement**. How ignorant! 2 Corinthians 10:12 (NLT)*

Jesus' earthly life is the standard by which we are to measure our lives. Comparing ourselves with anyone else is setting the bar too low. Ours is not the kind of race that is run as a competition against other people.

The Apostle Paul ministered much on the subject of fulfilling God's plan. A man who spent the early part of his life working against the plan of God, Paul wanted to be sure that once on God's side he didn't waste the precious opportunity that was his.

*But my life is worth nothing to me unless I use it for finishing **the work assigned me by the Lord** Jesus — the work of telling others the Good News about the wonderful grace of God. Acts 20:24 (NLT)*

*I have fought the good fight, I have **finished the race**, I have kept the faith. 2 Timothy 4:7*

Paul didn't live randomly, leaving things to chance. He was extremely focused. Perhaps his most passionate words on this subject are found in 1 Corinthians 9:24-27:

*Don't you realize that in a race everyone runs, but only one person gets the prize? So run to win! All athletes are disciplined in their training. They do it to win a prize that will fade away, but we do it for an eternal prize. So I run **with purpose in every step**. I am not just shadowboxing. I discipline my body like an athlete, training it to do what it should. Otherwise, I fear that after preaching to others I myself might be disqualified. (NLT)*

These great verses we have looked at contain many valuable lessons for us:
1. God has designed a race, or course for each individual, that only he or she can run.
2. Sin and unnecessary weights will slow or stall our progress.
3. We are only to compare ourselves with Jesus, not with other people.
4. Focused effort and discipline are necessary to stay on the path.
5. It's possible to know that you are on the right path.
6. It's possible to have been on the wrong path but still end up on course.

7. It's possible to know when you are approaching the finish line.

From Paul's writings, we can see that he considered the plan of God to be his highest priority. As we look at the words of Jesus, it's clear that He also highly esteemed the will and plan of God:

*And He said to them, "Why did you seek Me? Did you not know that **I must be about My Father's business**?" Luke 2:49 (NKJV)*

*Jesus said to them, "My food is to **do the will** of him who sent me and to **accomplish his work**." John 4:34*

*I glorified you on earth, having **accomplished the work** that you gave me to do. John 17:4*

*"Father, if you are willing, remove this cup from me. Nevertheless, **not my will, but yours**, be done." Luke 22:42*

Accomplishing God's will is a necessity for all of us, for He *needs* all who are in His body functioning in their place at full potential. As we remain close to Him, continually consecrating ourselves, we can discover and fulfill His plan for our lives. The enemy will surely try to distract and sidetrack us, but the believer who learns the Bible, develops their prayer-life, and is led by the Spirit, need not worry about missing God's will. God does not plan a course for you and then leave you on your own. He has provided great grace and help so you may know, run, and finish your race, and one day hear Him say:

Well done, good and faithful servant. You have been faithful over a little; I will set you over much. Enter into the joy of your master. Matthew 25:21

Confess this:

> ***I delight to do his will. I know His will for my life. I will stay on the path He's laid out for me, and I will finish my course with joy. When I cross the finish line I will be a winner. There is no greater success for me than doing His will.***

THE BLESSING

Christ hath redeemed us from the curse of the law, being made a curse for us: for it is written, Cursed is every one that hangeth on a tree: That the blessing of Abraham might come on the Gentiles through Jesus Christ; that we might receive the promise of the Spirit through faith.
Galatians 3:13-14 (KJV)

These are familiar verses to many Christians, and are most often used to proclaim the joyful fact that we are no longer under the curse. As important as it is to know what we've been redeemed *from*, these verses also tell us what we've been redeemed *to*. We've been redeemed *from* the curse but redeemed *unto* the blessing. In other words, our redemption didn't just take something bad away from us, it also added something wonderful to us that we didn't have before. More than just providing freedom from sickness, sin and poverty, redemption brought the blessing of the Lord into our lives.

The blessing of the LORD makes rich, and he adds no sorrow with it.
Proverbs 10:22

What is this blessing of the Lord? It is a divine empowerment for increase, and it's God's passionate desire that it flow in our lives. He has made great provision for it to do so.

*Blessed be the God and Father of our Lord Jesus Christ, who **has blessed us** in Christ with every spiritual blessing in the heavenly places.*
Ephesians 1:3

God is serious about blessing man. Think about His creation: the first thing Adam ever heard through his ears was the voice of God saying, "Be blessed! Multiply, increase, fill up the earth, etc." Adam obeyed that command and began operating just like His creator: speaking and seeing things come to pass. Adam named the animals so he could call them to work for him. Everything about the earth was made to respond to the blessing. Earth was perfect; quite different than we know it today.

When sin entered the earth, dramatic changes began to take place. Adam was forced to leave the garden, a flood covered the earth, and man's ability to speak like God was limited at the Tower of Babel. These changes were not just acts of judgment, they also were acts of mercy in which we see God still providing a measure of His blessing to man. Soon God made a covenant of blessing with a man named Abraham, who received God's promise and cooperated with it by faith. This blessing increased Abraham's life in every way. It protected him, gave him influence, allowed him to help others, brought him victory, helped him live long and strong, and made him very rich.

And I will make of you a great nation, and I will bless you and make your name great, so that you will be a blessing. I will bless those who bless you, and him who dishonors you I will curse, and in you all the families of the earth shall be blessed. Genesis 12:2-3

This blessing that Abraham had wasn't just for him, it belonged to all his offspring as well. When Christ died and redeemed us, He connected us to Abraham's blessing and made provision for it to flow in our lives.

And if you are Christ's, then you are Abraham's offspring, heirs according to promise. Galatians 3:29

We are instructed to look at Abraham's life as an example of what the blessing is like and then expect it to work in our lives just as it did in his.

*So then, those who are of faith **are blessed** along with Abraham, the man of faith. Galatians 3:9*

Notice that in the New Covenant, we are not trying to get *a* blessing, we already have *the* blessing – every spiritual blessing. The word *spiritual* indicates that everything that we receive from God is first received spiritually. We receive what He has given us in our spirits first, then we see it occur in the natural.

The blessing works in our lives in the same way that it worked in Abraham's life, by faith. God has embedded His blessing into the promises found in the Bible, and as our faith latches on to those promises and speaks them out, the blessing begins to run its course. I love how Peter describes this truth:

*According as his divine power hath given unto us **all things** that pertain unto life and godliness, through the knowledge of him that hath called us to glory and virtue: Whereby are given unto us exceeding great and precious promises: that by these ye might be partakers of the divine nature, having escaped the corruption that is in the world through lust. 2 Peter 1:3-4 (KJV)*

The blessing that's already ours manifests in our lives as we, by faith, receive and cooperate with God's promises. It should be understood that as with Abraham, this blessing creates increase over the course of our entire life, not all in one day. We are not to be discouraged if we don't see it all at once, but we should continue to agree with Paul's declaration in Romans 15:29:

I know that when I come to you I will come in the fullness of the blessing of Christ.

The *fullness* includes the blessing in all its forms, reaching into every area of our lives, even affecting those who are connected to us. And, it includes the highest form of the blessing of the Lord: "you will *be* a blessing."

Confession:

The blessing of the Lord is on me. It makes me rich in every way: spiritually, mentally, physically, materially. I'm blessed going out and coming in. I'm blessed to be a blessing.

HEALED

If you will diligently listen to the voice of the LORD your God, and do that which is right in his eyes, and give ear to his commandments and keep all his statutes, I will put none of the diseases on you that I put on the Egyptians, for I am the LORD, your healer. Exodus 15:26

This verse contains one of the great *I Am* names that God taught His people long ago. These covenant names reveal different attributes of His eternal character. The Hebrew words in this verse are *Jehovah Rapha*, meaning *The Lord who heals*. He *always has been* the Lord our healer, and He *always will be* the Lord our healer for He cannot change (see Malachi 3:6).

Let's look at the last phrase of this verse in some other translations:

I am the Lord, your life-giver. (Bible in Basic English)

I, the Lord, make you immune to them. (Goodspeed)

I love that last one. He makes me **immune**. Here's another great verse from the Old Testament that shows how committed He is to our physical health and well-being:

*Bless the LORD, O my soul, and forget not all his benefits, who forgives all your iniquity, who **heals all your diseases**. Psalm 103:2-3*

In the Old Testament, Israel had the benefit of a covenant of healing with God. He promised to heal them when they were sick, and then keep them well. The Old Testament is actually full of similar verses that reiterate the wonderful truth that God is a healer. What do healers do? They heal. You don't have to talk a dog into barking and you don't have to talk God into healing; it's His very nature. He loves healing.

Under the New Covenant, do we have a similar promise of healing? Not exactly. Under our covenant, which is called a better covenant, we have something even greater than God's promise to heal. Because Christ paid the price to redeem us from sickness and disease, healing is now more than a promise. It is an accomplished fact. Isaiah prophesied about this and *Young's Literal Translation* renders it most accurately:

*Surely **our sicknesses he hath borne, And our pains — he hath carried them**, And we — we have esteemed him plagued, Smitten of God, and afflicted. And he is pierced for our transgressions, Bruised for our iniquities, The chastisement of our peace [is] on him, And by his bruise there is healing to us. Isaiah 53:4-5*

The New Testament celebrates the fulfillment of this prophecy:

*This was to fulfill what was spoken by the prophet Isaiah: "**He took our illnesses and bore our diseases**." Matthew 8:17*

When did He take our illnesses? When He took our sin, at the cross. As He suffered for our transgressions and bought our freedom from the power of sin, He also suffered to redeem us from every sickness and every disease. If He bore sickness in His body, why should I bear it in my body? I shouldn't bear it; I must resist it.

Peter also makes reference to Isaiah's prophecy in one of his letters:

*He himself bore our sins in his body on the tree, that we might die to sin and live to righteousness. By his wounds **you have been healed**. 1 Peter 2:24*

To say we *have been* or *were* healed is to look back to something that happened in the past. If I *have been* healed, then I *am* healed. If I am healed, I'm well and strong. We're not waiting for God to do something about our sicknesses. He's waiting for us to find out about what He's already done for us and then take it by faith.

Why doesn't He just drop healing on us if we need it? He cannot, because it is our responsibility to receive. He can only extend to us the gift He's made available. We must reach out and take by faith what He has given to us by His grace.

We live in a world that has been corrupted by sin, where sickness and the devil are ever-present. Satan cares nothing about our rights in Christ, and he hopes we never discover what Jesus has done for us. When we understand all that is included in our redemption, it will be the end of Satan's domination over us.

*How God anointed Jesus of Nazareth with the Holy Spirit and with power. He went about doing good and **healing all** who were oppressed by the devil, for God was with him. Acts 10:38.*

*And Jesus went throughout all the cities and villages, teaching in their synagogues and proclaiming the gospel of the kingdom and **healing every disease and every affliction**. Matthew 9:35.*

The devil is the author of sickness, disease, and deformity, but Jesus is The Healer who is thrilled to heal *all*. After all, He's already paid the price to redeem us. Jesus was very aggressive against sickness and disease here on earth because He knew that He would be paying the ultimate price, fulfilling Isaiah's prophecy. Much of His earthly ministry included deliverance and healing for the sick. His ministry today is exactly the same. He was, is, and forever shall be the Lord, our healer. That makes us the healed of the Lord!

Confession:

> *He is the Lord who heals me, therefore I am the healed of the Lord. I claim immunity from sickness and disease. He bore my diseases; therefore, I do not need to bear them. He took my sicknesses; therefore, I will not take them. I refuse to accept sickness and disease. The Bible says that by His wounds I have been healed; therefore, I am healed now. Healing and health are mine today!*

I AM RICH

*You will be made **rich in every way** so that you can be generous on every occasion, and through us your generosity will result in thanksgiving to God. 2 Corinthians 9:11 (NIV)*

Rich is not a bad word, it's a Bible word. If a preacher tells you that God wants you to be rich, don't be offended. It doesn't mean that preacher is trying to line *his* pockets; he's trying to line *your* pockets. But first, you must agree with what God has said, instead of agreeing with the confusing things we hear Christians so often say about money.

The Bible does teach extensively about the dangers of covetousness. The Master Himself made this statement, which we embrace as much as we do any other scripture:

*And he said to them, "Take care, and be on your guard against **all covetousness**, for one's life does not consist in the abundance of his possessions." Luke 12:15*

Covetousness is a prosperity-killer. You and I must come to the place where our possessions mean nothing to us in comparison with the things of God. Then we must remain on guard to keep it that way. However, as we seek to walk in mastery over covetousness, we must not neglect to look at the other side of the truth: God wants you to be blessed exceedingly; He wants you to be rich. He said so. Why? One reason is so you can be used by Him to be a blessing to others.

*You know the generous grace of our Lord Jesus Christ. Though he was rich, yet for your sakes he became poor, so that by his poverty he could **make you rich**. 2 Corinthians 8:9 (NLT)*

Notice the redemptive language used in this verse. As He took our sins and sickness at Calvary, He also took our poverty so we could have His prosperity and provision. Just as God sees us with Christ's righteousness instead of our sin, He also sees us as having been made rich with the abundance and fullness that Jesus always has enjoyed with the Father. He sees us rich. He's made us rich.

Some people say that these scriptures are only referring to spiritual riches. That is not true. These verses actually are speaking primarily of money and material riches. Let's look at another verse in 2 Corinthians 9:

And God is able to make all grace abound to you, so that having all sufficiency in all things at all times, you may abound in every good work. 2 Corinthians 9:8

To *abound* means: *to overflow, to experience abundance, to have more than you need, to have too much.* This kind of abundance is mentioned in this favorite scripture of mine:

The thief comes only in order to steal and kill and destroy. I came that they may have and enjoy life, and have it in abundance (to the full, till it overflows). John 10:10 (AMP)

Some people may read this scripture and become excited, thinking, "God wants to help me get my bills paid." True, but *your* needs being met are the lowest form of prosperity. He wants you to be believing for the excess to be able to pay off other people's bills. That's where the real fun begins.

*Remember the words of the Lord Jesus, how he himself said, "It is **more blessed** to give than to receive." Acts 20:35*

God's will for every believer is that he or she would be rich. A good definition for rich is *a full supply.* When you are fully supplied, God can use you to be a supply to someone else. When the church begins a project, you are able to ask the Lord how much of that project He wants you to take care of. Does He want you to do half? Two-thirds? All of it? There is a church I know of that recently completed a building project costing over 50 million dollars. There is a businessman in that church who's vision is to pay off that building. He has already given millions into that building project. Friend, you just can't do that if you're poor.

Adopt this mindset: Being poor is bad. Being rich is good. (That doesn't mean poor *people* are bad. It's poverty that we are against, not people.)

Notice Abraham, our example of someone who had the blessing of the Lord:

*Now Abram was **very rich** in livestock, in silver, and in gold. Genesis 13:2*

Very rich. God was not only okay with it, He was the one who brought it to pass in Abraham's life. Let's refuse to put up with poverty and lack. Let's also put away small thinking. Stop feeling guilty about getting anything nice. Nice things aren't on the earth for crooks and drug dealers and the ungodly to have, they're here for God's kids. It grieves the Father when He is so rich but His children are broke.

Sure, there's a balance in this area, and some people have gotten money by questionable means. But you are well equipped in your relationship with God: you are able to remain balanced and correct in this area of your life, learning to prosper *His way*. Here's a verse that will help a rich person like you strike the proper balance:

As for the rich in this present age (that's me!), *charge them not to be haughty, nor to set their hopes on the uncertainty of riches, but on God, who **richly provides us with everything to enjoy.** 1 Timothy 6:17*

Confession:

I am rich. I'll never be broke again. He has made me rich in every area, in every way. I can be generous every time the opportunity to give arises. I abound to every good work, because I always have all sufficiency in all things at all times. I'm not poor. I'm not middle class. I am rich!

27

GOD LIVES IN ME

*To them God chose to make known how great among the Gentiles are the riches of the glory of this mystery, which is **Christ in you**, the hope of glory. Colossians 1:27*

You don't have to understand what *Christ in you* means to know it sounds really good. Surely it must give an advantage to the child of God. It certainly does. We are able to live a different kind of life than the unbeliever, and we really should not think of ourselves as merely human anymore. God lives in us, just as He did Jesus when He was on the earth (see Philippians 2). Jesus was a divine being that took on flesh, we are human beings that have taken on the divine. I'm not just a man, I'm a God-man.

*It is no longer I who live, but **Christ who lives in me**. Galatians 2:20*

These verses were a mystery to me when I first came across them. I wondered how Christ could live in me. I couldn't see how it was possible. We must understand though that the word *Christ* is not Jesus' last name; it means *anointed one*. He was Jesus, the Christ; Jesus, the Anointed One. We too are anointed ones. Christ, or the Anointed One, lives in us in the person of the Holy Spirit.

*If the Spirit of him who raised Jesus from the dead **dwells in you**, he who raised Christ Jesus from the dead will also give life to your mortal bodies **through his Spirit who dwells in you**. Romans 8:11*

Wow! I have a powerhouse in me. The Holy Spirit is the one who hovered over the face of the deep waiting for God to say, "Let there be light." He's the one who hovered over Mary and planted the seed of God in her womb. He was the fire in the burning bush, the still, small voice that Elijah heard, and everything all at once on the day of Pentecost. What's more, it was the life-giving power of the Spirit that raised Jesus from the dead. The Holy Spirit is living in us now, with all His experience, knowledge, and resurrection power. Amazing! No wonder John called the Holy Spirit the *Greater One*.

*You are from God, little children, and have overcome them; because **greater is He who is in you** than he who is in the world. 1 John 4:4 (NASB)*

God the Holy Spirit, is the Greater One. By contrast, that makes Satan the lesser one. The Spirit is the ever-victorious one; therefore, Satan is the eternally-defeated one. The Holy Spirit is the greatest success ever. Satan is the biggest loser ever.

Jesus spent much time teaching about the Spirit who was to come, giving us a preview of just how great the Spirit's work in the believer would be. Jesus spoke of *another* coming to help us; one who was just like Him.

*And I will ask the Father, and he will give you another Helper, to be with you forever, even the Spirit of truth, whom the world cannot receive, because it neither sees him nor knows him. You know him, for he dwells with you and **will be in you**. John 14:16-17*

Verse 16 in *The Amplified Bible* enlightens us further:

And I will ask the Father, and He will give you another Comforter (Counselor, Helper, Intercessor, Advocate, Strengthener, and Standby), that He may remain with you forever.

He's all that, *in me*. All that He is, He is *in me*. All the help He gave to Jesus, He'll give *to me*. This is some of the greatest news a person could ever receive! You might just want to give the Lord a shout right now!

*Do you not know that **you are God's temple** and that God's Spirit dwells in you? If anyone destroys God's temple, God will destroy him. For God's temple is holy, and you are that temple. 1 Corinthians 3:16-17*

The great benefits we receive from His indwelling presence also bring great responsibility on our part. God *Himself* lives in you, not just

His power and help. It is important that He's housed properly, in an environment worthy of His greatness. We are repeatedly warned in the scriptures to maintain proper standards of living, catering to His preferences.

*Or do you not know that **your body is a temple of the Holy Spirit within you**, whom you have from God? You are not your own, for you were bought with a price. So glorify God in your body. 1 Corinthians 6:19-20.*

We don't know how well the church at Corinth heeded the message the first time, but Paul was impressed to write it again in his next letter to the Corinthians:

*What agreement has the temple of God with idols? For **we are the temple of the living God**; as God said, "I will make my dwelling among them and walk among them, and I will be their God, and they shall be my people. Therefore go out from their midst, and be separate from them, says the Lord, and touch no unclean thing; then I will welcome you, and I will be a father to you, and you shall be sons and daughters to me, says the Lord Almighty." 2 Corinthians 6:16-18*

These verses don't require a lot of explanation. The message is plain and simple: you have to live right if you want to experience the benefits of His presence. Watch what you do with that body. Make lifestyle choices that are within the boundaries of the Bible, or you will distance yourself from His help. Let's do our part by living in a holy manner, and I guarantee that God will do His part by being everything that He is, in you.

Confess today the greatness of the Holy Spirit's work in you:

He lives in me. He dwells in me. He's my helper, my comforter, my counselor, my strengthener. The Greater One is in me, giving life to my body, enlightening my mind, and blessing my spirit with His presence. I am the temple of the Holy Spirit.

SUPERNATURAL PEACE

I have told you these things, so that in Me you may have [perfect] peace and confidence. In the world you have tribulation and trials and distress and frustration; but be of good cheer [take courage; be confident, certain, undaunted]! For I have overcome the world. [I have deprived it of power to harm you and have conquered it for you.]
John 16:33 (AMP)

Everyone wants peace, but peace can be defined many different ways. Society broadly uses the term to describe an absence of war. Yet most would agree that peace also is a highly sought commodity on a personal level. I'm happy when our country is at peace instead of at war, but I also want my own life to have a tangible peace instead of a sense of distress and frustration. In order to have that, it's necessary to get God's definition of peace, and pursue the kind of peace He describes and gives. Again, look at Jesus' words from the Amplified Bible:

Peace I leave with you; My [own] peace I now give and bequeath to you. Not as the world gives do I give to you. Do not let your hearts be troubled, neither let them be afraid. [Stop allowing yourselves to be agitated and disturbed; and do not permit yourselves to be fearful and intimidated and cowardly and unsettled.] John 14:27

This peace that comes from God is nothing like what the world thinks of as peace. It is a supernatural peace. The world's peace is totally dependent upon favorable circumstances. God's peace depends only on God Himself. The difference between the two is obvious. God never changes, so the peace He gives is constant. Circumstances never remain the same, so the world's level of peace is always changing.

This supernatural peace that the Bible speaks of is given to us when we receive Christ. It is part of our *welcome package*, when the Holy Spirit

31

comes to indwell us. The Bible refers to peace as a *fruit*, indicating that it can grow and develop.

But the fruit of the Spirit is love, joy, **peace***, patience, kindness, goodness, faithfulness. Galatians 5:22*

This peace is like nothing else. It is truly an inner peace – a peace that settles so deeply inside that it's difficult to describe to those who haven't experienced it. This peace can be sensed just as strongly in challenging times as it is in times of ease. Listen to Isaiah's description of the peace of God:

You keep him in **perfect peace** *whose mind is stayed on you, because he trusts in you. Isaiah 26:3*

The word *perfect* in the Hebrew language is actually also the word for peace. A literal rendering of this would be: "You keep him in peace-peace whose mind is stayed on you . . . . " Peace-peace sounds great to me – a double-dose of the God-kind of peace.

Do not be anxious about anything, but in everything by prayer and supplication with thanksgiving let your requests be made known to God. And **the peace of God, which surpasses all understanding***, will guard your hearts and your minds in Christ Jesus. Philippians 4:6-7*

I remember reading that verse early on in my Christian walk and thinking, "I wonder what that kind of peace would be like?" That peace was actually already in me, but I was ignorant of how to tap into it. I didn't realize that whether I experienced that kind of peace was up to me, not God. I since have learned how to walk in this peace that surpasses understanding, and I haven't gone a day without it for many years.

Have you noticed in the verses we've looked at to this point, how many things *we* are told to do in order to maintain this peace? For example, John 14:27 said *we* were not to let our hearts get agitated. Although this perfect peace resides in our born-again spirits, we must control our soul – our thoughts and feelings – and not allow them to override the peace of God.

For God is not a God of confusion but of peace. 1 Corinthians 14:33

Circumstances cannot steal our peace. However, if we choose to think about and meditate on our problems, instead of what God has said in the Bible, we will forfeit His peace and experience confusion. If you become overwhelmed and are in confusion, begin immediately to meditate on God's Word, which is the answer for every problem.

*And **let the peace of Christ rule in your hearts**, to which indeed you were called in one body. And be thankful. Colossians 3:15*

The Greek word translated as *rule* includes the thought of an umpire at a sporting event. You must umpire the thoughts and words that try to gain entrance into your mind. Many times you will have to act as a baseball umpire would, and call those thoughts "Out!", refusing to entertain them.

This peace is to be so constant in our lives that if it leaves, we know something is wrong. Determine to not allow anything to steal this supernatural peace. It is much too important. The peace of God is actually a constant manifestation of His presence in you, and the flow of that peace is one of the main ways that the Holy Spirit leads us in life.

*For you shall go out in joy and be **led forth in peace**. Isaiah 55:12*

If we stay close to the God of peace, He will always keep us in the peace of God.

Confession:

> *I let the peace of Christ rule in my heart. God's peace is already in me. I keep my mind on Him, and He keeps me in perfect peace. Circumstances may change, but they don't affect my peace. My peace remains constant because my faith is in Him. I follow peace.*

DIVINE JOY

I have told you these things, that My joy and delight may be in you, and that your joy and gladness may be of full measure and complete and overflowing. John 15:11 (AMP)

Christians ought to be the happiest people on earth. God wants us to be happy. He said so, and the text above gives us an easy two-step formula for divine joy. First, give attention to the things He has told us (His Word). Then, experience ever-increasing measures of His joy. You'll have His joy when you do things His way. If you don't, you won't. It really is that simple.

Religion would complicate things, even saying that God never promised us happiness. But Jesus distinctly mentioned "joy and delight...in full measure, complete, and overflowing." This joy should be visible in our lives. Even on a natural level, when something great happens at a sporting event, people's level of joy begins to exceed their ability to keep it in. They make all types of physical movements, and express that joy with their mouths. Both naturally and spiritually, real joy is visible.

Before I was saved, I was critical of the born-again people that I met. They always had a silly smile on their face for no apparent reason. I thought they were strange for being happy, and I thought I was normal by having the same sour look that everyone else had. Now I'm the one who goes around happy because I've been strengthened by the joy of the Lord.

And do not be grieved, for the joy of the LORD is your strength. Nehemiah 8:10

Like everything that proceeds from God, this joy is independent of natural circumstances. Christians have what it takes to be happy, even if natural circumstances do not warrant it. That explains why Paul made some of the statements he did in the word.

*Rejoice in the Lord **always**; again I will say, Rejoice. Philippians 4:4*

If Paul practiced this in his own life (as I'm sure he did), then we know that he found joy in some extremely difficult situations. For example, we know he was in more than one shipwreck where he spent considerable time in the water. How do you have happy feelings in those types of circumstances? Well, you aren't happy because you *feel* happy, you're happy because you've chosen to ignore your feelings and instead believe and act on the good news in God's Word. You're happy by faith. Here's how James described it:

*Count it **all joy**, my brothers, when you meet trials of various kinds. James 1:2*

I like how the *New Living Translation* says this:

*Dear brothers and sisters, when troubles come your way, consider it **an opportunity for great joy**. James 1:2 (NLT)*

If you have to *count it all joy*, then it probably doesn't feel very joyful. But if you really believe that God will bring you through to the other side, there is reason to be happy! That joy will work to turn things around, even ministering health to your body.

***A happy heart** is good medicine and **a cheerful mind** works healing, but a broken spirit dries up the bones. Proverbs 17:22 (AMP)*

Be happy and be healed!

When you really believe God's words in the face of opposing circumstances, a big smile comes to your face, and lightness fills your heart. It's no wonder that the scriptures encourage the strongest joy in the toughest times.

But rejoice, inasmuch as ye are partakers of Christ's sufferings; that, *when his glory shall be revealed, ye may be glad also with **exceeding joy**.* 1 Peter 4:13 (KJV)

The joy of the Lord is an exceeding joy. It will exceed and outlast any trouble we're in. When you and I make the effort to rejoice when we really feel like crying, it's an expression of faith, and it causes our problems to take a back seat to God's Word. It brings God's presence on the scene, and puts Him in a position to work good things in our lives.

*You make known to me the path of life; **in your presence there is fullness of joy**; at your right hand are pleasures forevermore. Psalm 16:11*

As strange as it sounds, we need to become *serious* about rejoicing, putting ourselves in remembrance of God's promises. We are not allowed to live in sadness. It's not acceptable to have down days and walk around depressed when the Greater One is inside of you! *Make yourself* express the joy that's already in you. Just put on a laugh or a dance, and it will activate that divine joy and will allow God to work a change in the situation.

*This is the day which the Lord has brought about; **we will rejoice and be glad in it**. Psalm 118:24 (AMP)*

We live in a day where there's not always much to be happy about in the natural. But the church is in a day that the Lord has brought about; it's a day of rejoicing. Faith-filled believers know that God's joy is to be a constant flow in their lives; a display to the world in tough times. Sometimes that joy bubbles to the top. At other times, we must rejoice by faith, as an act of our will. Either way, we are maintaining that flow of divine joy. And if we walk in joy, we will walk in victory!

Confession:

I will rejoice in Him at all times. Nothing can take my joy away. God's joy, the joy He Himself has, has been given to me and is in me now. That joy strengthens me as I give expression to it. I choose to rejoice today. Ha, Ha, Ha!

PROTECTED

Those who live in the shelter of the Most High will find rest in the shadow of the Almighty. This I declare about the Lord: He alone is my refuge, **my place of safety;** *he is my God, and I trust him. For he will rescue you from every trap and protect you from deadly disease. He will cover you with his feathers. He will shelter you with his wings.* **His faithful promises are your armor and protection.** *Psalm 91:1-4 (NLT)*

It doesn't matter where you live on this planet; if you are following God, you have a covenant of protection that out-performs any man-made security system. You should expect to be kept safe from evil and accidents. God has made provision on many levels for our safety. We are surrounded with protection.

Surely, LORD, you bless the righteous; you surround them with your favor as with a shield. Psalm 5:12 (NIV)

The shield that the Old Testament saints were familiar with was not just a round disc that they held in front of themselves, but one that covered them on every side. Their shield literally surrounded them. And so does ours: the shield of faith. We are surrounded with protection so the evil one cannot touch us.

My prayer is not that you take them out of the world but that you **protect them from the evil one.** *John 17:15 (NIV)*

In Jesus' great prayer in John 17, He petitioned the Father that we might experience all the benefits that He experienced while on earth. He wanted us to have the same degree of protection that He had. Most of us are not exposed on a daily basis to people who want to kill us like Jesus experienced, but if you are, be encouraged. You're covered. Notice how divine protection worked for Him.

37

*Again they sought to arrest him, but **he escaped from their hands**. John 10:39*

*So they were seeking to arrest him, but **no one laid a hand on him**, because his hour had not yet come. John 7:30*

*And they rose up and drove him out of the town and brought him to the brow of the hill on which their town was built, so that they could throw him down the cliff. **But passing through their midst**, he went away. Luke 4:29-30*

Jesus turned around and walked right through the middle of the crowd that was trying to throw Him off of a cliff. No one could get hold of Him. That's amazing protection. Every so often you see a football player who is so slippery and fast that no one can tackle him. Bodies are flying everywhere, grasping for the ball carrier, but that player goes right through them into the end zone. That's what Jesus did, except He wasn't running. He just walked right on through, and when His enemies grabbed for Him, they grabbed the power of God or an angel and just bounced right off. What wonderful protection!

Then you will walk on your way securely, and your foot will not stumble. Proverbs 3:23

Be confident that as you move about in the will of God, you have perfect protection. I don't have accidents. I'm not always stubbing my toes and hitting my head. I can fly, drive, ride, sail, etc. and claim protection as I do it. Calamity can't come near me.

Some Christians might think that kind of talk is arrogant. Others might reply, "I wouldn't say that if I were you." They are afraid of Murphy's Law and are afraid of the devil. They live by the phrase, "You never know what might happen." But I speak boldly about God's protection because I have His laws working for me. Anyone who thinks my confessions are out of line might faint if they heard some of the things David said before going out to the battlefield:

*A thousand may fall at your side, ten thousand at your right hand, but **it will not come near you**. Psalm 91:7*

What some might consider arrogance or irreverence is really just an honest expression of faith in God's protection. These expressions are necessary. A natural security system would be of no value if you didn't take time to set it before leaving the house. Likewise, we must arm our spiritual protection and security system. We set our alarm system with our mouths, talking about how He loves to protect us (review Psalm 91:2).

Does it work? Definitely. I've experienced God's mighty protection and so have you. We don't know of all the calamities we've missed; many never happened because of God's protection. The devil would love to kill us, and would do it in a second if he had the opportunity, but he hasn't killed us because he can't get to us.

*We know that God's children do not make a practice of sinning, for God's Son holds them securely, and **the evil one cannot touch them**. 1 John 5:18 (NLT)*

Make a practice of staying under His circle of protection. Don't get out from within your shield. He has assigned a security detail to you that will not fail: the angels, the blood of Jesus, the armor of God, the leading of the Holy Spirit, His promises in the Bible, etc.

We understand that good, sincere believers sometimes experience mishaps or tragedies. The reasons why may not always be clear, but you must realize that there was no failure on God's side. He will try to warn people to help keep them safe. So often when the enemy gets in, it's because we got out – out from under the place of perfect protection. Let's take the knowledge we have and remain covered with God's feathers and sheltered with His wings.

Confession:

I have divine protection surrounding me everywhere I go. I only go where I have peace to go. I listen to warnings and promptings from the Holy Spirit. The wicked one can't touch me. I always get to the other side and arrive alive. God alone is my refuge and place of safety. He's my shield on every side.

LOVE

Three things will last forever—faith, hope, and love—and the greatest of these is love. 1 Corinthians 13:13 (NLT)

Is there anything really more important than your faith? Yes. There would be no faith without love. How so? Without love there's no God, for the Bible declares, "God is love." And without God, you could pretend to have all the faith in the world but it would be useless since our faith and trust is in Him.

There's another reason why love is foundational to our faith: if we are not convinced of His intense love for us, how could we ever trust Him enough to operate in faith? The reason you and I can step out and boldly believe something different than what we see is because we believe that His love for us is strong enough to never let us down.

*So we have come to know and to **believe the love that God has for us**. God is love, and whoever abides in love abides in God, and God abides in him. 1 John 4:16*

God is love. Find out what love will do, and you'll know what God will do.

*Even before he made the world, **God loved us and chose us** in Christ to be holy and without fault in his eyes. God decided in advance to adopt us into his own family by bringing us to himself through Jesus Christ. This is what he wanted to do, and it gave him great pleasure. Ephesians 1:4-5 (NLT)*

His amazing love has been directed toward you longer than the world has existed, and you just heard about it fairly recently. God has been waiting for thousands of years for you to be born so He could express His love to you. How sad it is that some people never allow Him to do it. His love for us is so vast that we must have His help just to understand it.

And may you have the power to understand, as all God's people should, how wide, how long, how high, and how deep his love is.
Ephesians 3:18 (NLT)

We've all seen shows where a single person finally finds that right one, and tears of joy are shed as they realize they were made for each other. That's how God sees you; you're the one He's been waiting so long to find. You're the one that completes Him. I know that can be difficult to believe, but we must "believe the love that God has for us."

The love of God is of a different variety than the so-called love we find in the world. The world loves things based on how those things make *them* feel. If you make me feel wonderful, then I love you, etc. That's not real love, that's selfishness. The love of God is a committed love that simply seeks the highest and best for the other person regardless of how he or she makes you feel. Look at this great description of the love of God:

Love is patient, love is kind. It does not envy, it does not boast, it is not proud. It is not rude, it is not self-seeking, it is not easily angered, it keeps no record of wrongs. Love does not delight in evil but rejoices with the truth. It always protects, always trusts, always hopes, always perseveres. Love never fails. 1 Corinthians 13:4-8 (NIV)

These verses show how God is acting toward us today. He won't fail us, because love never fails. He loves us unconditionally – irrespective of our performance. Although it's freely given, His love is not without obligation. He does ask for a few things in return.

And he (Jesus) said to him, "You shall love the Lord your God with all your heart and with all your soul and with all your mind. This is the great and first commandment. And a second is like it: You shall love your neighbor as yourself. On these two commandments depend all the Law and the Prophets." Matthew 22:37-41

God wants us to take the love that He has displayed towards us and love Him back. Then, He asks us to take that same love and use it on other people. Fortunately, we have a rich supply of that love already in us.

*And hope does not put us to shame, because **God's love has been poured into our hearts** through the Holy Spirit who has been given to us. Romans 5:5*

Therefore be imitators of God, as beloved children. And walk in love, as Christ loved us and gave himself up for us, a fragrant offering and sacrifice to God. Ephesians 5:1-2

If we are walking in love toward other people, then we will be patient and kind, not rude and obnoxious. We won't hold grudges, and life won't completely revolve around us anymore. Isn't that exciting? It actually is very exciting when we have a revelation of the importance of walking in love.

Owe no one anything, except to love each other, for the one who loves another has fulfilled the law. Love does no wrong to a neighbor; therefore love is the fulfilling of the law. Romans 13:8,10

People tried for centuries to fulfill the law, but only Jesus was able to do it. You and I, however, need only to walk in love to be counted as having kept the law perfectly. *Then* the blessings of obedience are ours. *Then* our faith will work. And, as we express God's love toward other people and see the results in their lives, we will become increasingly convinced of the intensity of His love for us.

Confess this today:

I have known and do believe that God loves me. He has loved me forever, and now shows it. I'm a receiver of His great love. His love has been poured out toward me and in me. I walk in love. I treat people right. I seek their good, not my own. Because love never fails and I walk in love, I never fail!

SOWING AND REAPING

He also said, "This is what the kingdom of God is like. A man scatters seed on the ground." Mark 4:26 (NIV)

Just like our natural world has physical laws (such as gravity) that we must learn to flow with, there is a spirit-world, which is governed by spiritual laws. That spirit-world is called the Kingdom of God. It refers to the realm of God's rule or domain, His government, His way of doing things, His laws. Jesus thought it essential to teach about how God's Kingdom works, enabling His followers to function efficiently in it. Without a doubt, the main law of the Kingdom is sowing and reaping. Speaking once again of the Kingdom, Jesus said:

It is like a grain of mustard seed, which, when sown on the ground, is the smallest of all the seeds on earth, yet when it is sown it grows up and becomes larger than all the garden plants and puts out large branches, so that the birds of the air can make nests in its shade. Mark 4.31-32

We see the following laws and truths established in the Bible:
1. Regardless of how small or insignificant things may look, they can become bigger than you ever expected.
2. Within itself, the seed has the code (or blueprint) for it to expand and change forms, becoming the very thing it represents.
3. The seed is inactive until placed in the ground.
4. Time must pass between seedtime and harvest.
5. The condition and maintenance of the ground is of utmost importance.

The sower sows the word. Mark 4:14

Here's where sowing and reaping becomes exciting. As we plant the seed of God's Word in the ground of our hearts, and we keep that seed watered through repeated hearing and meditation, that Word expands and multiplies in us until it has changed things around us, producing a harvest in our lives. It works every time, just like the natural laws of sowing and reaping. Farmers aren't shocked when the seed they planted comes up. They know how to work the laws of farming, and they know the laws work.

Do to others whatever you would like them to do to you. This is the essence of all that is taught in the law and the prophets. Matthew 7:12 (NLT)

Think about this: *anything* you plant, positively or negatively, is something you're going to see again – multiplied. Look at Galatians 6:7-9:

*Do not be deceived: God is not mocked, for **whatever one sows, that will he also reap**. For the one who sows to his own flesh will from the flesh reap corruption, but the one who sows to the Spirit will from the Spirit reap eternal life. And let us not grow weary of doing good, for in due season we will reap, if we do not give up.*

The Phillips Translation of verse 7 reads:

*A man's harvest in life will depend **entirely** on what he sows.*

Don't complain about your life. You have what you have been sowing, nothing else. If you find yourself surrounded with difficult people, I'd suggest taking a look back to see how you have treated people over the years. If you don't like the harvest you see, start planting different seed. Thankfully, we can change our own lives purposely by changing what kind of seed we sow. Think of what kind of harvest you want in every area of your life, and continually sow good seed in those areas.

Our finances are an area where we want the laws of sowing and reaping to work on our behalf.

Give, and it shall be given unto you; good measure, pressed down, and shaken together, and running over, shall men give into your bosom. For with the same measure that ye mete withal it shall be measured to you again. Luke 6:38 (KJV)

Church people love to talk about the financial harvest they're expecting, but they often haven't planted any seed. I'm all for an overwhelming financial harvest, but that means there was some substantial seed sown. Paul left no doubt that the concept of sowing and reaping applies to the area of our finances.

The point is this: whoever sows sparingly will also reap sparingly, and whoever sows bountifully will also reap bountifully. Each one must give as he has decided in his heart, not reluctantly or under compulsion, for God loves a cheerful giver. And God is able to make all grace abound to you, so that having all sufficiency in all things at all times, you may abound in every good work. 2 Corinthians 9:6-8

What if you don't have a financial seed to sow? You can believe that God will give you some seed. Just make sure that when it comes in, you plant it. Don't eat (or spend) the seed you are supposed to plant.

He who supplies seed to the sower and bread for food will supply and multiply your seed for sowing and increase the harvest of your righteousness. 2 Corinthians 9:10

What you do is coming back to you! So purpose to generously and regularly sow good things so you have good, regular harvests coming in.

Confession:

> *I reap what I sow. Therefore I sow only good things. I am friendly, so I have friends, I'm a blessing to others, so blessings come to me. I give generously, so people are always giving to me. I am looking for my harvest and I will reap because I don't give up! God is bringing me good seed to sow.*

EMPOWERED

But you will receive power when the Holy Spirit has come upon you, and you will be my witnesses in Jerusalem and in all Judea and Samaria, and to the end of the earth. Acts 1:8

The Spirit of God comes to live in the believer at the salvation experience, but there is also an experience called the Baptism in the Holy Spirit, where He comes *upon* the believer. That experience is easily received by faith, and includes the evidence of speaking in other tongues. Every believer needs to be empowered in such a manner and walk in the reality of it throughout his or her life.

*And behold, I am sending the promise of my Father **upon you**. But stay in the city until you are clothed with power from on high. Luke 24:49*

This was not an optional experience. Jesus' disciples were instructed not to go *anywhere* without this power. We see in the scripture that the empowerment of the Spirit is ultimately for a purpose beyond ourselves. We have the Spirit *in* us to help us and bless us, but He comes *upon* us so He can bring His help and blessing to others. Jesus said that this power would make us witnesses: divinely enabled representatives of Him. As we obey the commission to go preach the gospel, we are to expect power, signs, and wonders to accompany the message.

*And **these signs** will accompany those who believe: in my name they will cast out demons; they will speak in new tongues; they will pick up serpents with their hands; and if they drink any deadly poison, it will not hurt them; they will lay their hands on the sick, and they will recover. So then the Lord Jesus, after he had spoken to them, was taken up into heaven and sat down at the right hand of God. And they went out and preached everywhere, while **the Lord worked with them** and confirmed the message by accompanying signs. Mark 16:17-20*

He ascended and sat down so we could take up the power that's ours and get to work. Too often we focus our Christianity only on ourselves, forgetting that we have been anointed to represent Him to the world around us. Let us go forth in His power and anointing, being mindful also to draw upon His love and compassion. It was compassion for the lost that often moved Jesus to act and bring a flow of power on the scene.

And Jesus went throughout all the cities and villages, teaching in their synagogues and proclaiming the gospel of the kingdom and healing every disease and every affliction. When he saw the crowds, he had compassion for them, because they were harassed and helpless, like sheep without a shepherd. Then he said to his disciples, "The harvest is plentiful, but the laborers are few" Matthew 9:35-37

We've been empowered to duplicate His ministry. Notice from the above verses what His ministry included:

1. Preaching the gospel. People cannot believe and receive what they have not heard.

2. Healing. The same God that saves also heals. We can bring healing through the laying on of hands at the same time we bring the gospel message to someone.

3. Teaching and discipleship. The phrase "sheep without a shepherd" indicates that when we bring people to Jesus, we must also help them find their pastor and local church. They must be taught and matured or they will not succeed in their Christian life.

Jesus lived conscious of the empowerment of the Spirit in His life. So must we. As the Spirit anointed Jesus to minister, He will also anoint and help us.

The Spirit of the Lord is upon me, because he has anointed me to proclaim good news to the poor. He has sent me to proclaim liberty to the captives and recovering of sight to the blind, to set at liberty those who are oppressed, to proclaim the year of the Lord's favor. Luke 4:18-19

It's not difficult to find people who are oppressed and held captive by the enemy. They are everywhere, and they need what we have. Jesus isn't going to personally come tell them the good news and set them free; that's our job. He has anointed us to accomplish it. I love how the early church took this power and ran with it.

Now many signs and wonders were regularly done among the people by the hands of the apostles. And more than ever believers were added to the Lord, multitudes of both men and women, so that they even carried out the sick into the streets and laid them on cots and mats, that as Peter came by at least his shadow might fall on some of them. The people also gathered from the towns around Jerusalem, bringing the sick and those afflicted with unclean spirits, and they were all healed. Acts 5:12, 14-16

When power flowed through those who were anointed, great numbers were added to the Lord. This picture from the book of Acts is not some special sovereign move of God that was just for that day, it's the blueprint for the church age in which we live. If we don't see this today like they did then, something's wrong, and it's not on God's side. He's placed His Spirit in us and upon us, and sent us. When you see Jesus' followers in the pages of scripture doing His works, see yourself right there with them. We have the same Holy Spirit that they did, and the same assignment from the Master Himself.

Truly, truly, I say to you, whoever believes in me will also do the works that I do; and greater works than these will he do, because I am going to the Father. John 14:12

"Whoever" includes you and me. Let's get to work, doing His works!

Regularly make this confession:

I am anointed. The Spirit of the Lord is upon me. I have His healing power with me wherever I go, and I'm ready to minister it to anyone who will take it. I am an anointed witness, bringing good news to this world that so desperately needs it. If Jesus or His followers did it in the Bible, I can do it by the Holy Spirit's anointing.

I HAVE A SUPPLY

And my God will supply every need of yours according to his riches in glory in Christ Jesus. Philippians 4:19

The Christian who is growing in the things of God will take interest in the works that God is raising up. Your local church, missionaries, and other ministries, all of which are advancing the Kingdom, need to be supported. God wants you involved, doing your part. The only problem is, He often will ask you to do things that are beyond your ability to accomplish with the resources you presently have. Why would God do that? He wants you to use your faith. That's the only way He can become involved, and He doesn't like to be excluded.

But without faith it is impossible to please Him: for he who comes to God must believe that He is, and that He is a rewarder of those who diligently seek Him. Hebrews 11:6 (NKJV)

If God asks you to do something, and you don't know where the money is going to come from, don't feel as though you may not have heard God correctly. This type of situation is characteristic of Him. He's not setting you up for failure; He wants you to know that you have a supply.

God once asked Abraham to sacrifice His only son, symbolic of God the Father's offering of Jesus. Isaac was old enough to know about sacrifices, and was concerned that a major part of this one was missing: the offering.

*And Isaac spake unto his father and said, My father: and he said, Here am I, my son. And he said, Behold the fire and the wood: but where is the lamb for a burnt offering? And Abraham said, My son, **God will provide** himself a lamb for a burnt offering: so they went both of them together. Genesis 22:7-8 (KJV)*

Those three words, "God will provide" are some of the strongest words in the Bible. What great faith is displayed here. Notice also where it said, "they went both of them together." Faith will make movement before all the answers are evident. Start doing what you can. When someone says, "I see that you have these things in motion, but where's the money coming from?" you can answer, "God will provide. I have a supply." How did things work out with Abraham and Isaac?

And Abraham lifted up his eyes and looked, and behold, behind him was a ram, caught in a thicket by his horns. And Abraham went and took the ram and offered it up as a burnt offering instead of his son. So Abraham called the name of that place, "The Lord will provide"; as it is said to this day, "On the mount of the Lord it shall be provided." Genesis 22:13-14

He has mountains of provision for you and me, too, and we're already on the mountaintop of supply, seated with Him in heavenly places.

I believe that when Abraham said "God will provide," a ram had a sudden urge to change course and go investigate the nearby thicket. Likewise, when you give a faith-answer to the needs in your life, your supply begins moving toward you. It's a spiritual version of "supply and demand." God has a supply for me, and my faith makes a demand on it. We must stop seeing the need as a negative thing. It's just an opportunity for God to bring His supply to our lives. There would be no divine supply, if there was not a need.

Therefore I tell you, do not be anxious about your life, what you will eat or what you will drink, nor about your body, what you will put on. Is not life more than food, and the body more than clothing? Look at the birds of the air: they neither sow nor reap nor gather into barns, and yet your heavenly Father feeds them. Are you not of more value than they? Matthew 6:25-26

Jesus goes on to talk about how God clothes the flowers, and then sums up the teaching with this great verse:

*But seek first the kingdom of God and His righteousness, and **all these things** will be added to you. Matthew 6:33*

He's trying to establish us in the truth that, if we live in the will of God, we have a divine supply that will wipe out every need that comes up in life. If we depart from God's will, we leave that supply. If we put the world's way of doing things first, we limit ourselves to the economy of the world. Go God's way and have His supply. Operate in faith by speaking things that agree with the Bible. Talk about how much God loves to take care of you and supply for you. Does the Bible actually teach that? Yes!

*If you then, who are evil, know how to give good gifts to your children, **how much more** will your Father who is in heaven give good things to those that ask him! Matthew 7:11*

God loves to supply for His children more than any good father in this world ever loves to take care of his kids. But, there also is a devil, who will work to cut off your supply. If you sense delay, don't hesitate to use your authority over the devil. Command him to take his hands off of your supply, then send the angels to do their part. They stand ready to exercise a positive influence in your situation, causing your supply to come.

Are they not all ministering spirits, sent forth to minister for them who shall be heirs of salvation? Hebrews 1:14 (KJV)

Don't be satisfied going without. Make a demand on your supply today.

Here are some of the things I like to confess about my supply:

Just like the birds that fly through the sky, I have a Father, and He's my supply.
Just like the flowers, all dressed up so fair, I have a supply of the best clothes to wear.
My father loves to take care of me. The angels are working for me. All the money shall come. I go where He leads, and He supplies all my needs!

MY WORDS COME TO PASS

Have faith in God. For verily I say unto you, That whosoever shall say unto this mountain, Be thou removed, and be thou cast into the sea; and shall not doubt in his heart, but shall believe that those things which he saith shall come to pass; **he shall have whatsoever he saith.** *Mark 11:22-23 (KJV)*

This verse is either true or it's not true. I believe it is true, and my life thus far has proven that it's true. So has yours. Regardless of whether you have purposefully practiced this verse, the *law of saying* has been working for you. If you take an honest look at your life right now, you'll notice that it is a reflection of the words that you have spoken in days and years past. Don't like what you see? Start changing what you say.

My heart is stirred by a noble theme as I recite my verses for the king; **my tongue is the pen of a skillful writer.** *Psalm 45:1 (NIV)*

How is the tongue a pen? Your tongue takes the Word of God, and writes it on the tablet of your heart (see Proverbs 7:2-3.) When negative words are spoken over and over, and they become etched in one's spirit, those words move the person's life in a negative direction. The momentum of those words is not quickly changed. Likewise, positive, purposeful, and scriptural words that have been engraved on the heart will propel that life in the direction of those words. Your words set the course for your life.

*For we all often stumble and fall and offend in many things. And if anyone does not offend in speech [**never says the wrong things**], he is a fully developed character and a perfect man, able to control his whole body and to curb his entire nature. James 3:2 (AMP)*

James goes on to illustrate the power of the tongue by comparing it to the rudder of a ship, or a bit in the mouth of a horse. What do a rudder and a bit have in common? They are both instruments that establish direction, like the steering wheel on a car. Your tongue is steering your life, giving coordinates and mapping a course. Because there is so much power in the tongue, it is of great importance that we continually monitor our mouths. The Book of Proverbs admonishes us to do so, describing both the positive and negative effects of the words we speak.

The words of the reckless pierce like swords, but the tongue of the wise brings healing. Proverbs 12:18 (NIV)

From the fruit of their lips people enjoy good things, but the unfaithful have an appetite for violence. Those who guard their lips preserve their lives, but those who speak rashly will come to ruin. Proverbs 13:2-3 (NIV)

A gentle tongue [with its healing power] is a tree of life, but willful contrariness in it breaks down the spirit. Proverbs 15:4 (AMP)

*From the fruit of his mouth a man's stomach is filled; with the harvest from his lips he is satisfied. **The tongue has the power of life and death**, and those who love it will eat its fruit. Proverbs 18:20-21 (NIV)*

Words can kill, and they can heal. Your words will chart a course for your life, either according to the will of God, or in opposition to it. Is it any wonder that many of the writers of the New Testament emphasized controlling the tongue?

*Those who consider themselves religious and yet **do not keep a tight rein on their tongues** deceive themselves, and their religion is worthless. James 1:26 (NIV)*

When a person properly controls his or her tongue, the purposeful use of words sets good things in motion in his or her life. This is what Jesus was talking about when He said, "He shall have whatsoever he says." Jesus didn't just teach about this, He practiced it. Right words were His habit. Here's a simple example of how His words worked for Him:

*One day he got into a boat with his disciples, and he said to them, "**Let us go across to the other side** of the lake." So they set out. Luke 8:22*

Those who are familiar with this story know that all hell came against them to try and sink them in the middle of the lake. Many might underestimate the importance of the Master's words here, saying, "Jesus was just letting them know where He wanted to go." Exactly! His words were giving the heading. And where did they end up? At the bottom of the lake? No, thank God they went to the other side, just like He said. Jesus didn't treat His words casually, nor should we.

I tell you, on the day of judgment people will give account for every careless word they speak. Matthew 12:36

God created this world with words of faith. Jesus spoke faith-words and went "to the other side" every time. When He told us to have faith in God, He was letting us know that our words can create our reality, and bring us to the other side of every situation in life. We are to expect our words to come to pass, just as Jesus did. Don't talk about what the situation looks like; say what you want it to be. Say what God says.

*Since we have the same spirit of faith according to what has been written, "I believed, and so I spoke," **we also believe, and so we also speak**. 2 Corinthians 4:13*

God's Word forms beliefs within us. We put His words in our mouths, and they become indelibly written upon our spirits. Then, in times of test or trial, those words rise up to our minds. As we speak and hold fast to those words, they will certainly come to pass!

Confession:

I have what I say. My words set the course for my life. I am careful to say only what I want, because what I say is what I will have. I believe God's Word; therefore I only speak in agreement with it, never against it. What I say is coming my way!

PRAYER HEARD = PRAYER ANSWERED

*Whatever you ask in my name, this will I do, that the Father may be glorified in the Son. If you **ask me anything** in my name, I will do it. John 14:13-14*

The Greek word translated as *ask* in these verses is very interesting. It's not the kind of asking that hopes *maybe* it will be rewarded; it's the kind that fully expects the answer. For example, if I ask my children to do a chore around the house, I don't go away wondering whether or not it will be done. My request leaves them no option. My authority in my house gives me the right to make such demands. Likewise, God has invited us to ask things of Him that leave Him no option but to accommodate us.

*If you abide in me, and my words abide in you, **ask whatever you wish, and it will be done** for you. John 15:7.*

Religion does not recognize these scriptural truths, but teaches instead that God, being sovereign, reserves the right to deny or grant any given request. That may sound spiritual, but it certainly is not scriptural. The New Testament leaves no question that although the *power* for answered prayer lies with God, the *responsibility* for it lies with us.

*Your Father knows what you need before **you** ask him. Matthew 6:8*

Yes, He knows our needs, but action on our part is still required. We must ask. There can be no answer to prayer when no prayer is offered. Since our needs are ongoing, asking must be practiced with regularity. Jesus continued this teaching in Matthew 7 where He showed that we are to ask, not ritually, but habitually.

Keep on asking and it will be given you; keep on seeking and you will find; keep on knocking [reverently] and [the door] will be opened to

55

you. For everyone who keeps on asking receives; and he who keeps on seeking finds; and to him who keeps on knocking, [the door] will be opened. Matthew 7:7-8 (AMP)

Many incorrectly interpret this verse, believing that we are to repeat the same request over and over again before the Lord. Jesus was simply teaching that we are to maintain the habit of asking. We ask His blessing over our food *every time* we eat, because each meal needs to be blessed, but we don't keep repeating our request from breakfast throughout the day. He heard us the first time, and if He hears once, it is sufficient.

*If my people who are called by my name humble themselves, and pray and seek my face and turn from their wicked ways, then **I will hear** from heaven and will forgive their sin and heal their land. 2 Chronicles 7:14*

I'm thankful that He's a God who hears. People of other religions pray, but their false gods aren't capable of hearing. God can and does hear; yet He doesn't hear every person nor does He hear every prayer. The Apostle John's writings bring us great clarity where cooperating with God in prayer is concerned.

And this is the confidence (the assurance, the privilege of boldness) which we have in Him: [we are sure] that if we ask anything (make any request) according to His will (in agreement with His own plan), He listens to and hears us. 1 John 5:14 (AMP)

He hears us *if* we ask according to His will. If that's true, we must conclude that He does not hear us if we ask against His will. Knowing His will before going to prayer is essential. How do we know His will? The main way He reveals His will to us is through His Word. His Word is His will. When you pray in agreement with the Word, you know you will be heard.

And if (since) we [positively] know that He listens to us in whatever we ask, we also know [with settled and absolute knowledge] that we have [granted us as our present possessions] the requests made of Him. 1 John 5:15 (AMP)

Let this verse renew your thinking. Most only believe they have their answer by looking to see if the natural circumstances have changed. But this scripture teaches that we are to believe we have our answer once we know He has heard us. *If we know He hears, we know we have.* Did you ask according to His will? If so, you are to consider yourself to be presently in possession of your answer. What if God decides not to answer? He does not have that option, because He cannot violate His promise to us to answer when He hears. What John wrote is in agreement with Jesus' words on this subject:

*Therefore I say unto you, What things soever ye desire, **when ye pray, believe that ye receive them,** and ye shall have them. Mark 11:24 (KJV)*

First we believe we receive, then we have. This is the law of faith, believing what God says, rather than what we see.

*If any of you lacks wisdom, let him ask God, who gives generously to all without reproach, and it will be given him. But **let him ask in faith,** with no doubting, for the one who doubts is like a wave of the sea that is driven and tossed by the wind. For that person must not suppose that he will receive anything from the Lord. James 1:5-7*

The one who prays in faith will receive. He receives *when he prays,* which is another way of saying he receives when God hears. Our prayers aren't burdensome to the Lord when they are prayed in faith. Asking for the things we need was His idea. He delights in the faith-filled prayer because it's a prayer He can answer, so come boldly and come often!

*In that day you will ask nothing of me. Truly, truly, I say to you, whatever you ask of the Father in my name, he will give it to you. Until now you have asked nothing in my name. **Ask, and you will receive, that your joy may be full.** John 16:23-24*

Confession:

> **God hears me when I pray. I pray according to His will, in agreement with His word.**
> **I believe I receive when I pray, and I will have my answer. If I know He hears, I know I have.**

THE RENEWED MIND

Do not be conformed to this world (this age), [fashioned after and adapted to its external, superficial customs], but be transformed (changed) by the [entire] renewal of your mind [by its new ideals and its new attitude], so that you may prove [for yourselves] what is the good and acceptable and perfect will of God, even the thing which is good and acceptable and perfect [in His sight for you]. Romans 12:2 (AMP)

When we come to Christ, we bring along wrong thinking, and must immediately begin the process of mind-renewal. Similar to the programming of a computer, our thought-life, having been programmed by the world, must receive a transformation via input from God. The Greek word for *transformed* is actually the word we know as *metamorphosis*, meaning a complete change. Are our minds really in such bad shape that they need a complete overhaul? Emphatically yes.

*For **the mind that is set on the flesh** is hostile to God, for it does not submit to God's law; indeed, it cannot. Those who are in the flesh cannot please God. Romans 8:7-8*

It's not necessarily the bad habits like smoking or overeating that are the main indicators of someone who is *in the flesh*, but wrong thinking. Carnality is primarily a condition of the mind. Thoughts born from the flesh lead to struggle and defeat, but no one who walks in the light with a renewed mind has ever ended up in failure. To leave the mind unrenewed is the biggest favor any Christian can do for the enemy. It makes his job easy, allowing him free access in our lives.

*Now this I say and testify in the Lord, that you must no longer walk as the Gentiles do, in **the futility of their minds**. They are darkened in their understanding, alienated from the life of God because of the ignorance that is in them, due to their hardness of heart. Ephesians 4:17-18*

We don't want to be distanced from the power and life of God through ignorance and wrong thinking. Paul goes on to give us the remedy:

*To put off your old self, which belongs to your former manner of life and is corrupt through deceitful desires, and to **be renewed in the spirit of your minds**, and to put on the new self, created after the likeness of God in true righteousness and holiness. Ephesians 4:22-24*

An unrenewed mind keeps us captive in this natural world with its backward way of doing things. In contrast, the renewed mind allows us to live beyond the natural, in the spirit and in success, realizing our domination and victory over the devil. Let's study how this transformation takes place.

*For this is the covenant that I will make with the house of Israel after those days, declares the Lord: **I will put my laws into their minds**, and write them on their hearts, and I will be their God, and they shall be my people. Hebrews 8:10*

It's not through prayer or the laying on of hands that the mind becomes renewed; it happens only as God's laws are put into our minds. This happens as we take His laws (His words) and input them into our minds. As we feed our spirits on the Word of God, the Word will wash out the old thinking, replacing it with new thoughts, God-thoughts.

For my thoughts are not your thoughts, neither are your ways my ways, declares the LORD. For as the heavens are higher than the earth, so are my ways higher than your ways and my thoughts than your thoughts. Isaiah 55:8-9

*For, "Who can know the Lord's thoughts? Who knows enough to teach him?" But we understand these things, for **we have the mind of Christ**. 1 Corinthians 2:16 (NLT)*

Although we have God's thoughts, the renewing of the mind is not just a one-time event. Continual input of God's Word is necessary throughout the course of one's life, in order to maintain a successful thought-life. The mind is where battles are won and lost, and there always will be pressure from the natural realm to entice us to conform, thinking according to what we see, hear, and feel. We must exercise vigilance in order to keep our minds focused on what God said.

We destroy arguments and every lofty opinion raised against the knowledge of God, and **take every thought captive** *to obey Christ. 2 Corinthians 10:5*

Recognize wrong thoughts when they come and refuse to allow them to stay. Use the scriptures to kick them out of your mind right away, like a bouncer would kick undesirable people out of a bar. It's *your* job to control your thought-life, not God's. He has equipped you, and will strengthen you to keep a firm grip on your mind.

For God did not give us a spirit of timidity (of cowardice, of craven and cringing and fawning fear), but [He has given us a spirit] of power and of love and of **calm and well-balanced mind** *and discipline and self-control. 2 Timothy 1:7 (AMP)*

We understand, of course, that we do not completely control what kind of thoughts come to us, but we can totally control whether those thoughts remain within us. A deliveryman could randomly bring anything in his truck to my door, but if I didn't order it, I won't sign for it. As long as we are in this world, thoughts of every kind will come our way, but we only accept and meditate upon those thoughts that agree with God.

Finally, brothers, whatever is true, whatever is honorable, whatever is just, whatever is pure, whatever is lovely, whatever is commendable, if there is any excellence, if there is anything worthy of praise, **think about these things**. *Philippians 4:8*

Confess this:

> *I am in control of my mind. I only meditate on what is godly. I have the mind of Christ. I think God-thoughts. As I walk in the light, my mind becomes renewed. I think right, believe right, and live right. The discipline of my mind brings me success.*

LIVING LONG AND STRONG

*With **long life** I will satisfy him and show him my salvation. Psalm 91:16*

It's God's will that each of His children live a long time here on this earth; not just long chronologically, but long in productivity. He wants us to have a high-quality life with an abundance of strength and much fruit.

*The thief comes only in order to steal and kill and destroy. I came that they may have and enjoy life, and have it **in abundance** (to the full, till it overflows). John 10:10 (AMP)*

The Greek word translated as *abundance* means *superabundant in quantity, and superior in quality*. The abundance of God should manifest in all areas of our lives, including the area of our physical health and longevity. It is a sign to those in the world around us when we live year after year without bearing the curse of sickness in our bodies. It is a testimony to those who come after us when we finish our full course in life and die at a good old age without sickness and disease.

*Abraham lived for 175 years, and **he died at a ripe old age, having lived a long and satisfying life**. He breathed his last and joined his ancestors in death. Genesis 25:7-8 (NLT).*

Abraham's strength, health, and longevity are part of the blessing on his life that we have inherited through faith. Can we expect to live 175 years? That's highly unlikely. In Abraham's day, the world was still adjusting to the effects of the curse on the earth, and, although life spans were on the decline, they were still at higher levels than we see today. God had spoken of this decrease in the length of man's days, giving us the maximum number of years anyone could probably expect to live in our day under the Blessing of the Lord.

*Then the LORD said, "My Spirit shall not abide in man forever, for he is flesh: **his days shall be 120 years**." Genesis 6:3*

You may not know anyone who is 120 years old, but do you know that there are people on the earth today who are that old? Those who study human physiology tell us that our bodies, under the right conditions, are capable of living about that long. Now, God is not requiring us to all live until age 120, He specified only that we are to live until we are satisfied. If you are satisfied at 80, fine. If not, talk with Him about going on further, until you are satisfied. We don't want any empty, fruitless years, so we will need to contend for the life and strength of God at every age and stage.

Who satisfies your mouth [your necessity and desire at your personal age and situation] with good so that your youth, renewed, is like the eagle's [strong, overcoming, soaring]! Psalm 103:5 (AMP)

I will not die; instead, I will live to tell what the Lord has done. Psalm 118:17 (NLT)

Many people erroneously believe that our life span is predetermined by God and cannot be changed. Some even misquote scriptures, endeavoring to prove that we all have an appointed time to die. Here's one such verse that is often incorrectly quoted:

*And just as it is appointed for man **to die once**, and after that comes judgment. Hebrews 9:27*

This does not teach that there is a date circled on God's calendar when we must die; it says that we are only destined to die *one time*. Can a person die more than once? Absolutely. All are destined to die physically, unless Jesus comes first, but the scriptures also speak of the second death – an eternal, spiritual death. All who are in Christ will miss the second death, Praise God! The truth is, there is a *season* (not a date) when it is right to go home, and that time period shouldn't be in your 40's, 50's, 60's, or even 70's. God teaches us that there are things we can do to increase or decrease our longevity.

For "Whoever desires to love life and see good days, let him keep his tongue from evil and his lips from speaking deceit; let him turn away from evil and do good; let him seek peace and pursue it. 1 Peter 3:10-11

Hear, my son, and accept my words, that the years of your life may be many. Proverbs 4:10

*Children, obey your parents in the Lord, for this is right. "Honor your father and mother"—which is the first commandment with a promise—"so that it may go well with you and that **you may enjoy long life on the earth**." Ephesians 6:1-3 (NIV)*

*My child, never forget the things I have taught you. Store my commands in your heart. If you do this, **you will live many years**, and your life will be satisfying. Proverbs 3:1-2 (NLT)*

*"You must serve only the Lord your God. If you do, I will bless you with food and water, and I will protect you from illness. There will be no miscarriages or infertility in your land, and **I will give you long, full lives**. Exodus 23:25-26 (NLT)*

All of these verses promise long life, but notice that the promises are all conditional, requiring the fulfillment of obligations on our part. What are some of our obligations?

1. Watching what comes out of our mouth (walking in love).
2. Practicing righteousness, not evil.
3. Following the peace of God (being led by the Spirit).
4. Being a student of the word (doing His word and His will).
5. Treating those who are over us with honor and respect.

I plan to do these things, so I can live out my full lifespan here on earth, accomplishing the will of God, and leaving satisfied.

Confess this many times:

He satisfies me with a long, full, complete life.

CLOSE TO HIM

For I am sure that neither death nor life, nor angels nor rulers, nor things present nor things to come, nor powers, nor height nor depth, nor anything else in all creation, will be able to separate us from the love of God in Christ Jesus our Lord. Romans 8:38-39

Our lives are to be so intertwined with God that our enemies can't tell the difference between Jesus and us. Never will my enemies be able to get me off by myself to take advantage of me. My life is too wrapped up in God's life. Nothing presently going on in my life is powerful enough to unwrap me from Him, and nothing in the future will have that power either. There's too much of God on me and in me for the devil to defeat me.

*And **ye are complete in him**, which is the head of all principality and power. Colossians 2:10 (KJV)*

For too many years, I believed that I was incomplete. Even though the Bible teaches otherwise, I retained an outsider-mentality. That kind of thinking robbed me by keeping me distanced from the things of God. How it would have helped me to receive the revelation that from God's view, I can't be any closer to Him than I already am. I am part of the *in* crowd: I'm in Him and He's in me.

*To the praise of the glory of his grace, wherein **he hath made us accepted in the beloved**. Ephesians 1:6 (KJV)*

I'm accepted, I'm complete, and I can't be separated from Him. People may not accept me, even Christians may sometimes look down on me, but God will never do that. We should never think of ourselves as unworthy. No, we don't deserve any of the good things we receive from God, but He has made us worthy through Jesus' precious blood, bringing us close to Himself.

*Remember that you were at that time separated from Christ, alienated from the commonwealth of Israel and strangers to the covenants of promise, having no hope and without God in the world. But now in Christ Jesus **you who once were far off have been brought near by the blood of Christ**. Ephesians 2:12-13*

Verse 19 of this same chapter lets us know just how close we now are.

*Therefore you are no longer outsiders (exiles, migrants, and aliens, excluded from the rights of citizens), but you now share citizenship with the saints (God's own people, consecrated and set apart for Himself); and **you belong to God's [own] household**. (AMP)*

We're in the house! I know people love the Old Testament verse (Psalm 84:10) about how it's better to be a doorkeeper in the house of God than to dwell in the tents of the wicked, but don't look at yourself as the doorkeeper. We're in the New Covenant now. We've been brought inside, not even as servants, but as sons! Take your place of sonship and act like an insider, not an outsider. If I go to my parent's house and want something to eat, I just help myself. I know who I am. Because I'm a son, not a visitor, anything in the refrigerator is available for me. Likewise, in God's house we're residents, not visitors. I don't want to leave, I never have to leave, and nothing can make me leave.

*I give them eternal life, and they will never perish, and no one will snatch them out of my hand. My Father, who has given them to me, is greater than all, and **no one is able to snatch them out of the Father's hand**. John 10:28-29*

No one can snatch us, because they can't get to us. We are off-limits!

*And do not grieve the Holy Spirit of God [do not offend or vex or sadden Him], by Whom **you were sealed (marked, branded as God's own, secured)** for the day of redemption (of final deliverance through Christ from evil and the consequences of sin). Ephesians 4:30 (AMP)*

I like that it says we are marked, branded, and sealed. Our life in God is like one of those jelly jars with the pressurized lid. That lid keeps the jam protected and preserved from the outside elements. I guarantee that there's no devil strong enough to pry the lid of the Holy Spirit off of our lives! The Holy Spirit is always in us and with us, and we are sealed in Him.

Keep your life free from love of money, and be content with what you have, for **he has said, "I will never leave you nor forsake you."** *Hebrews 13:5*

Teach these new disciples to obey all the commands I have given you. And be sure of this: **I am with you always**, *even to the end of the age. Matthew 28:20 (NLT)*

I am His and He is mine. This great relationship benefits both God and us, for He desires our fellowship as much as we desire His.

That which we have seen and heard we proclaim also to you, so that you too may have fellowship with us; and indeed **our fellowship is with the Father and with his Son Jesus Christ.** *1 John 1:3*

God has done everything possible to bring us close to Himself. Yet, many believers act as though they only run into Him once a week. He's with us and in us all the time, so let's learn to acknowledge His glorious presence, fellowshipping with Him throughout the day. The more we look to Him, the more aware of Him we become. This enables us to draw upon more of His wisdom and life. Spend all day, every day, with God. It's why we've been brought close, and it's what blesses Him most.

Confession:

> *I am accepted in Him. He has made me complete, filling me with Himself. I can't be separated from Him or all He has. I am marked for life. I am branded as His own. He is always with me. I enjoy close fellowship with the Father. His blood has brought me near. I'm in the house!*

THE CERTAINTY OF THE WORD

*It seemed good and desirable to me, [and so I have determined] also after having searched out diligently and followed all things closely and traced accurately the course **from the highest to the minutest detail** from the very first, to write an orderly account for you, most excellent Theophilus, [My purpose is] that **you may know the full truth and understand with certainty and security against error** the accounts (histories) and doctrines of the faith of which you have been informed and in which you have been orally instructed. Luke 1:3-4 (AMP)*

*For truly, I say to you, until heaven and earth pass away, **not an iota, not a dot**, will pass from the Law until all is accomplished. Matthew 5:18*

If a person won't believe God's Word, I can't help them. If they won't believe the Word, God can't help them. All our divine help originates in God's Word. The Word is our answer. If you know the Word, you know enough to overcome any situation. People may ask, "Is God really asking us to believe, as absolute fact, words that were written in a book thousands of years ago?" He is, and that's why He took such care, using writers like Luke, to preserve it for us. He continues today to guard His Word, looking for the opportunity to bring it to pass in our lives.

*Then said the Lord to me, You have seen well, for **I am alert and active, watching over My word to perform it**. Jeremiah 1:12 (AMP)*

God's Word is not going anywhere. It has no expiration date. It will outlast anyone on the earth, and it will outlast any problem here on earth.

*For "All flesh is like grass and all its glory like the flower of grass. The grass withers, and the flower falls, but **the word of the Lord remains forever**." And this word is the good news that was preached to you. 1 Peter 1:24-25*

The early disciples had no other message but the Word, and every preacher since has been given the divine assignment of preaching the written Word of God.

Preach the word; be ready in season and out of season; reprove, rebuke, and exhort, with complete patience and teaching. 2 Timothy 4:2

Why are we to be such sticklers for the Word? It's the only thing that God has promised to back up with His power.

*Then the disciples went out and preached everywhere, and the Lord worked with them and **confirmed his word** by the signs that accompanied it. Mark 16:20 (NIV)*

All of God's power and ability reside in His Word in seed form. When those words are planted in a person's heart, they begin to explode into action on the inside of that person.

For as the rain and the snow come down from heaven and do not return there but water the earth, making it bring forth and sprout, giving seed to the sower and bread to the eater, so shall my word be that goes out from my mouth; it shall not return to me empty, but it shall accomplish that which I purpose, and shall succeed in the thing for which I sent it. Isaiah 55:10-11

There is a greater possibility of your grass not needing to be mowed after a week of rain, than there is of the Word not coming to pass when you put it to work in your life. You can be sure of the Word.

*So men are called gods [by the Law], men to whom God's message came—and **the Scripture cannot be set aside or cancelled or broken or annulled**—John 10:35 (AMP)*

Never will you stand on the Word to have it break or give way underneath you. There is no such thing as a broken scripture. They all work.

And we also thank God constantly for this, that when you received the word of God, which you heard from us, you accepted it not as the word

68

*of men but **as what it really is, the word of God, which is at work in you believers**. 1 Thessalonians 2:13*

The Word will never disappoint, but it doesn't work all by itself. We must believe it, feeding upon it until it convinces our heart and flows from our mouths. Think of the Word as faith-food, for it has been given to us for the purpose of forming our beliefs.

*Now Jesus did many other signs in the presence of the disciples, which are not written in this book; but **these are written so that you may believe** that Jesus is the Christ, the Son of God, and that **by believing you may have** life in his name. John 20:30-31*

If I believe, I have. It's that simple. People often complicate things, but God has made it easy to understand. If He said it, He'll do it, period. He has not given Himself a way out, but He has bound Himself to His Word forever.

God is not a man, that he should lie, or a son of man, that he should change his mind. Has he said, and will he not do it? Or has he spoken, and will he not fulfill it? Numbers 23:19

Become a Word-junkie. Many people take cigarette breaks throughout the day, so I think it's right for the believer to slip away every so often for his Word-fix. After all, the Word will fix any problem, and will break down every wall of resistance in our lives.

Is not my word like fire, declares the LORD, and like a hammer that breaks the rock in pieces? Jeremiah 23:29

Confess this today:

> *I will never encounter a problem that's too big for the Word. The Word is my answer and my help. I always ask, "What does the Word say?" His Word comes to pass in my life. I feed on His Word and speak His Word, and He stands ready to perform His Word that I'm standing on.*

MY FAITH WORKS

And Jesus answered them, "Have faith in God." Mark 11:22

Most reference Bibles point out that this scripture in the original Greek language reads: "Have the faith *of* God," or, as the *Bible In Basic English* renders it, "Have God's faith." Jesus told us to have the same kind of faith that God has and uses. Does God, the All-Powerful, operate by faith? Without a doubt.

By faith we understand that the universe was created by the word of God, so that what is seen was not made out of things that are visible. Hebrews 11:3

Faith deals with things that are not yet seen. God, in creation, operated the laws of faith to bring the world into existence. Those laws are simple: believe it, say it, and don't change (waver or doubt). We can do that as well. We do the believing and He does the performing.

And blessed is she that believed: for there shall be a performance of those things which were told her from the Lord. Luke 1:45 (KJV)

Your faith works just as God's did in creation and Jesus' did with the fig tree. Your faith is a measure of the same faith that He has. He doesn't do things one way and then ask us to do the same things using inferior equipment. No, we take the faith He's imparted to us at salvation and develop it through hearing, meditating, and speaking the Word.

So faith comes from hearing, and hearing through the word of Christ. Romans 10:17

The more we hear a thing, the more we are persuaded of it. Once we are convinced of the truth, faith is present and can be used – released into the earth through action. Does this sound absurd? It does to the multitudes of believers who are ignorant of this most basic truth. But really, every Christian should be familiar with the laws of faith, for their faith has already produced for them the greatest miracle that man can receive – the new birth.

*For by grace you have been saved **through faith**. And this is not your own doing; it is the gift of God, not a result of works, so that no one may boast. Ephesians 2:8-9*

It wasn't our power that caused us to pass from death to life spiritually. No one could produce that kind of resurrection power but God. However, what He graciously provides as a gift must still be received by our faith. Romans chapter 10 shows us how this simple process works:

*Because, if you confess with your mouth that Jesus is Lord and believe in your heart that God raised him from the dead, you will be saved. For **with the heart one believes** and is justified, and **with the mouth one confesses** and is saved. Romans 10:9-10*

We believe with the heart, and confess with the mouth. This isn't just a formula to become born-again, it's how we can receive any promise that God has extended to us, such as those concerning physical healing or financial provision. Your faith has already successfully received some of God's promises, and as long as you feed and exercise it, it will continue to see you through to victory in every situation.

*And he said to her, "Daughter **your faith has made you well**. Go in peace. Your suffering is over." Mark 5:34 (NLT)*

If her faith made her well, my faith can make me well. More than just an important ingredient in receiving, faith is actually *the determining factor* in whether a person receives from God. Although many emphasize the will or power of God, Jesus always emphasized the faith of the believer when helping others receive the answer to their needs.

The spirit often throws him into the fire or into water, trying to kill him. Have mercy on us and help us, if you can." What do you mean, 'If I can'?" Jesus *asked. **"Anything is possible if a person believes.** " Mark 9:22-23 (NLT)*

Notice that the man tried to lay the responsibility for his help on Jesus, but Jesus immediately pointed back to the man's faith. Here's another great example:

*And as Jesus passed on from there, two blind men followed him, crying aloud, "Have mercy on us, Son of David." When he entered the house, the blind men came to him, and Jesus said to them, "Do you believe that I am able to do this?" They said to him, "Yes, Lord." Then he touched their eyes, saying, **"According to your faith be it done to you.** " Matthew 9:27-29*

Although He is more than able, it is the expression of our faith that brings a flow of His ability and power to the situation. How important and precious our faith is. Learn to bring your faith to every challenge in life and you will be victorious in those challenges. Let's follow the example of others, like Jesus, Paul, and Abraham – the father of faith. The following passage is one of my favorites in the Bible concerning faith, for it shows how Abraham stood firm in the face of adversity to receive what God had said to him:

*As it is written, "I have made you the father of many nations"—in the presence of the God in whom he believed, who gives life to the dead and **calls into existence the things that do not exist.** In hope he believed against hope, that he should become the father of many nations, as he had been told, "So shall your offspring be." He did not weaken in faith when he considered his own body, which was as good as dead (since he was about a hundred years old), or when he considered the barrenness of Sarah's womb. No distrust made him waver concerning the promise of God, but he grew strong in his faith as he gave glory to God, **fully convinced that God was able to do what he had promised.** Romans 4:18-21*

Confession:

> *I believe God. He's put His faith in me, and that faith works for me just like it did for Abraham and countless others. I hear the Word, and I believe it and speak it. I refuse to change, therefore the circumstances have to change! I become what I believe.*

72

SUCCESS

*Thanks be to God, who in Christ **always leads us in triumphal procession**, and through us spreads the fragrance of the knowledge of him everywhere. 2 Corinthians 2:14*

Because every word in the Bible was chosen with precision and purpose, we understand that there are no false statements or exaggerations in the teachings of scripture. So, when a word as absolute as *always* is used, it is to be taken literally. Always – every single time – God leads us to triumph. We are never ordained to failure. We always win.

*In the Messiah, in Christ, **God leads us from place to place in one perpetual victory parade**. Through us, he brings knowledge of Christ. Everywhere we go, people breathe in the exquisite fragrance. 2 Corinthians 2:14 (MSG)*

Everywhere you go, success is there waiting for you. You are a success waiting to happen. And, your continued success is to be a testimony to those around you. When they look at your life, they should be impressed with God and desire Him. How is such success attainable? Only through obedience and faith.

*For everyone who has been born of God overcomes the world. And **this is the victory that has overcome the world— our faith**. 1 John 5:4*

The most notable success stories are those in which the greatest opportunities for failure existed. Those who attained great success often had to overcome tests, trials, and many obstacles that tried to block their way. We don't get thrilled when a test shows up, but we also know that there are no testimonies without tests, just as there are no victories without battles. We must have the proper mindset about the difficulties that come our way, knowing that we are predestined to succeed.

73

*No, in all these things we are **more than conquerors** through him who loved us. Romans 8:37*

If we will do things God's way, we will come out of every test on top. Regardless of how bad it looks in the natural, there is a way out. Our job is to work with God, learning to follow Him to the other side of the trouble.

No temptation has overtaken you except what is common to humanity. God is faithful and He will not allow you to be tempted beyond what you are able, but with the temptation He will also provide a way of escape, so that you are able to bear it. 1 Corinthians 10:13 (HCSB)

I often hear this verse misquoted as people religiously exclaim, "God said He wouldn't put more on us than we can bear." Please read it again. It does not say that. It says, in essence, that regardless of the type of test you find yourself in, He will provide the way of escape, the way out. That means you can beat it; you can whip it. The Greek word translated *bear it*, means *to bring up from underneath*. That sounds like a winning proposition to me.

But thanks be to God, Who gives us the victory [making us conquerors] through our Lord Jesus Christ. 1 Corinthians 15:57 (AMP)

Develop a winning mentality. Become like David who, when faced with a giant that wanted to kill him, ran as fast as he could – not away from the problem, but toward it. He knew that his covenant with God would cause him to prevail over the giant. Failure was not an option. The Bible is filled with many such success stories. One of the most encouraging is the story of Joseph. He faced several low spots in life, but always rose to the top. Even as a prisoner who was falsely accused, Joseph enjoyed success.

*The keeper of the prison paid no attention to anything that was in Joseph's charge, because the LORD was with him. **And whatever he did, the LORD made it succeed**. Genesis 39:23*

Those familiar with the story know that Joseph went from the prison to the palace, administering all the resources of Egypt, and ultimately protecting his own people in the time of famine.

*And we know that for those who love God **all things work together for good**, for those who are called according to his purpose. Romans 8:28*

Success is not difficult, as so many people believe, but it doesn't happen accidentally. Success always comes when we follow the plans that God lays out for us. Failure comes when we choose a path of our own design. It's easier to live in success than failure.

*This Book of the Law shall not depart from your mouth, but you shall meditate on it day and night, so that you may be careful to do according to all that is written in it. For **then you will make your way prosperous, and then you will have good success**. Joshua 1:8*

God's Word brings success, for there is no failure in it. Do the Word and live in the Word, and victory will be yours. You never have to fail and you never have to fall. Meditation (thinking and speaking the Word) will lead you into obedience to God's plan for your life, and fulfilling His will is success in its highest form.

If success has eluded you in the past, be encouraged today. Your knowledge of the Word will cause things to turn out for your good. Life will get better and better until you know nothing but victory.

*But the path of the righteous is like the light of dawn, which **shines brighter and brighter** until full day. Proverbs 4:18*

Confession:

I confess today that I always triumph in Christ. He leads me from victory to victory.
I am a winner – a success waiting to happen. Like Joseph, whatever I do succeeds.

STEADFAST FAITH

*Therefore, my beloved brothers, **be steadfast, immovable,** always abounding in the work of the Lord, knowing that in the Lord your labor is not in vain. 1 Corinthians 15:58*

Faith doesn't quit; that's all there is to it. It always gets up to fight another day. It reads the same verses, confesses the same verses, and rejoices over the same verses, knowing that it's impossible for the Word to fail. If we don't quit, we always win. If we quit, we never win.

Do not, therefore, fling away your fearless confidence, for it carries a great and glorious compensation of reward. Hebrews 10:35 (AMP)

The theme presented in these verses is: *"Don't quit. Don't give up."* Some have misconstrued faith to mean there will be no difficult spots in life. While it's true that faith and obedience can help us avoid many kinds of trouble, we will still encounter plenty of opposition while in this world. And, regardless of who you are, there will be times when you are tempted to give up and just forget about this whole faith thing. That's why we're told to remain steadfast, not casting away our confidence. The manifestation of our answer is attached to our ability to keep going. Look at the next verse:

*For you have need of **steadfast patience and endurance,** so that you may perform and fully accomplish the will of God, and thus receive and carry away [and enjoy to the full] what is promised. Hebrews 10:36 (AMP)*

If every test were a short one, the Lord would not need to repeatedly encourage us to hold on and keep going. Like it or not, sometimes the test goes on for a while. The reason why may or may not be apparent, but we do know that these tests can be good for us.

*Moreover [let us also be full of joy now!] let us exult and triumph in our troubles and rejoice in our sufferings, knowing that pressure and affliction and hardship **produce** patient and unswerving endurance. And endurance (fortitude) **develops** maturity of character (approved faith and tried integrity). And character [of this sort] **produces** [the habit of] joyful and confident hope of eternal salvation. Such hope never disappoints or deludes or shames us.... Romans 5:3-5 (AMP)*

Notice that the test is producing something *in* you and *for* you. Those who have lived for a while can confirm that as life progresses, bigger tests come along. But these bigger tests can actually seem smaller if we constantly and consistently show up to fight the good fight of faith. A great man of God once said, "I can believe God for a million dollars today easier than I could believe Him for one dollar years ago." The tests he endured in the early years of his life helped produce what would be necessary for his later life. You could say that the problems that seemed to be working against him were really working for him.

*That is why we never give up. Though our bodies are dying, our spirits are being renewed every day. For our present troubles are small and won't last very long. Yet **they produce for us** a glory that vastly outweighs them and will last forever! So we don't look at the troubles we can see now; rather, we fix our gaze on things that cannot be seen. For the things we see now will soon be gone, but the things we cannot see will last forever. 2 Corinthians 4:16-18 (NLT)*

We must focus on the right thing. Looking at the problem doesn't solve the problem, but instead magnifies it in our lives. We must focus on the answers found in the Word, fixing our gaze on things that are not seen. By faith we see the answer and believe we have it now. Doing this day after day while facing opposing circumstances requires steadfast endurance.

For we walk by faith, not by sight. 2 Corinthians 5:7

Our ability to persevere, staying in faith throughout the trial, affects the outcome of the situation much more than the circumstances themselves affect it. God's power can bring the necessary change to any situation, but it only works as we steadfastly maintain our position of trust in Him.

*For we have come to share in Christ, if indeed we **hold our original confidence firm to the end**. Hebrews 3:14*

Be a strong finisher. Be consistent and tenacious, for it will be necessary. Don't ever give up and surrender to the test. What if Joseph had allowed discouragement to overtake him while spending month after month in prison? Joseph was under a great trial, and won that trial by refusing to accept his surroundings as the final word. He stayed steadfast, trusting in what God had said to him.

*He had sent a man ahead of them, Joseph, who was sold as a slave. His feet were hurt with fetters; his neck was put in a collar of iron: until what he had said came to pass, **the word of the LORD tested him**. Psalm 105:17-19*

What if Moses had quit while in the desert for forty years, and the wilderness for another forty? What if Abraham had given up and stopped believing for his son during the twenty-five long years it took for it to come to pass? Let's follow their example, and we'll have their results.

*Then you will not become spiritually dull and indifferent. Instead, you will follow the example of those who are going to inherit God's promises **because of their faith and endurance**.... Abraham waited patiently, and he received what God had promised. Hebrews 6:12,15*

Confession:

> *I will not quit. I will not be defeated. I focus only on what God has said, and I will have what He has said. My problems are working for me. God is faithful to take me to the other side of every test, trial, circumstance, or situation.*

FREEDOM FROM FEAR

*That we, being delivered from the hand of our enemies, **might serve him without fear**, in holiness and righteousness before him all our days. Luke 1:74-75*

The devil is counting on Christians to be afraid of him, and most Christians are. That fear gives him the power he needs to keep people in bondage. But Jesus came to completely redeem us from all that would hold us captive. Because of that redemption, we can live every day of our lives free from fear.

*And also that He might **deliver and completely set free** all those who through the [haunting] fear of death were held in bondage throughout the whole course of their lives. Hebrews 2:15 (AMP)*

Fear keeps people in bondage. It sets the boundaries of their lives, and posts a guard at those boundaries so that they never go past them. Fear is a force – a powerful spiritual force – and if you allow it to make decisions for you, you will constantly back down from all that God wants you to do. There is another force called faith that will push out that fear and allow you to break through all of life's limitations.

But the just shall live by faith...and if he draws back and shrinks in fear, My soul has no delight or pleasure in him. Hebrews 10:38 (AMP)

What a stern warning. God tells us that it is not acceptable for His children to give in to fear and to back down in adversity. Thankfully, the next verse shows God's confidence in us. He believes that you and I will learn not to yield to fear, but instead to operate in faith.

But we are not of those who shrink back and are destroyed, but of those who have faith and preserve their souls. Hebrews 10:39

Fear can be so strong in a person's life, that they live in constant torment. I had experienced that kind of bondage in my own life, but have been free for so long now that I don't think of those days very often. What brought me out? The knowledge of the Word of God. His Word strengthened my spirit and provided the faith necessary to push out the fear. Today, as I stay full of the Word and the Spirit, fear is kept at a distance, and I abide in the love of God where there is no fear.

*There is no fear in love [dread does not exist], but full-grown (complete, perfect) love **turns fear out of doors and expels every trace of terror!** For fear brings with it the thought of punishment, and [so] he who is afraid has not reached the full maturity of love [is not yet grown into love's complete perfection]. I John 4:18 (AMP)*

You cannot keep fear from showing up at times, but you can control whether you yield to it. We must adopt scriptural thinking that understands that it's not acceptable to be afraid. You are not permitted to yield to fear when it comes. Fear at any level is unacceptable, and will actually draw what you dread to you. Refuse to tolerate fear.

*Even though I walk through the valley of the shadow of death, **I will fear no evil**, for you are with me; your rod and your staff, they comfort me. Psalm 23:4*

He said to them, "Why are you so afraid? Have you still no faith?" Mark 4:40

***Do not be afraid** of the terrors of the night, nor the arrow that flies in the day. **Do not dread** the disease that stalks in darkness, nor the disaster that strikes at midday. Psalm 91:5-6 (NLT)*

*Though a mighty army surrounds me, **my heart will not be afraid**. Even if I am attacked, I will remain confident. Psalm 27:3(NLT)*

*God is our refuge and strength, a very present help in trouble. Therefore **we will not fear** though the earth gives way, though the mountains be moved into the heart of the sea. Psalm 46:1-2*

He is not afraid of bad news; his heart is firm, trusting in the LORD. His heart is steady; he will not be afraid. Psalm 112:7-8

*And **do not [for a moment] be frightened or intimidated in anything** by your opponents and adversaries, for such [constancy and fearlessness] will be a clear sign (proof and seal) to them of [their impending] destruction, but [a sure token and evidence] of your deliverance and salvation, and that from God. Philippians 1:28 (AMP)*

As we see from these (and many other) verses, there is no good excuse in the sight of the Lord for being afraid. Earthquake, flood, lack, attack, disease, bad report, etc. may all be good excuses in the sight of man, but not before God. We must overcome fear the way Jesus overcame the storm that was sinking His boat: by resisting and rebuking it.

*So be subject to God. **Resist the devil [stand firm against him], and he will flee from you.** James 4:7(AMP)*

Anything that produces fear is of the devil, not of God, therefore resist fear just like you would stand against the devil in any other area. Do it in faith, and the Bible says the devil will flee. That fear will leave. Peace will come. The truth of God's Word will rise up strong within you, and you will walk right through the feelings of fear into the rejoicing of faith.

Fear can be an overwhelming force, but it also can manifest in more subtle forms, which we know as anxiety and worry. We must resist every temptation to fear and, as we do, panic, terror, and anxiety will be weapons that cannot prosper against us.

*Casting **all** your anxieties on him, because he cares for you. 1 Peter 5:7*

Confession:

I will not fear. I refuse to worry. I am not allowed to fear. Perfect love has cast fear out of my life. I am free from fear because God loves me, and He's with me.

GOD-TALK

For one who speaks in a tongue speaks not to men but to God; for no one understands him, but he utters mysteries in the Spirit. 1 Corinthians 14:2

The benefits of speaking in other tongues are among the greatest conferred upon the New Testament believer. The ability to commune and communicate with God on His level is priceless, for the limitations of our intellect and knowledge are bypassed. We tap into God's omniscience as we move into the realm of the spirit – the realm of answers, direction, and light. Things that are mysteries – unknown and unclear to us – can be handled in prayer with precision. Look how some other scholars translated *mysteries*.

He utters secret truths and hidden things [not obvious to the understanding]. (AMP)

In spirit, he is speaking sacred secrets. (RTHM)

What are these mysteries and secrets? Things concerning your future, things concerning situations and people you know, and situations and people that you don't know. These unknown things are mysteries to us, but not to God. He knows and understands all, but He requires the participation of the members of His body here on earth for Him to bring these things to pass. The one who will take time to pray in other tongues, speaking forth *sacred secrets*, is of great use to God.

*For if I pray in tongues, **my spirit is praying**, but I don't understand what I am saying. Well then, what shall I do? **I will pray in the spirit**, and I will also pray in words I understand. I will sing in the spirit, and I will also sing in words I understand.*
1 Corinthians 14:14-15 (NLT)

When we speak in other tongues (or *in the spirit*), our tongue becomes the instrument of our spirit instead of the instrument of our mind. We hook our tongue to our hearts, speaking from our spirit the utterances of the Holy Spirit. When Paul said, "I will pray…" he was helping us see that, as an act of the will, we can choose to speak in tongues at any time, just as we could choose to speak in our native language. Although we may sometimes sense a strong urge to pray, we do not need to wait for such a leading. Prayer in other tongues must become a habit with us, as it was with Paul.

I thank God that I speak in tongues more than all of you. 1 Corinthians 14:18

Daily time spent speaking in other tongues can affect many things, both in the spiritual and natural worlds. Sometimes the results of your prayers will be recognizable. At other times, you will sense the help of the Spirit in prayer, but never know what it was all about. Be satisfied knowing that if you yielded to Him, great things were accomplished.

Likewise the Spirit helps us in our weakness. For we do not know what to pray for as we ought, but the Spirit himself intercedes for us with groanings too deep for words. Romans 8:26

Our biggest weakness in prayer is our lack of knowledge of what to pray for. Thank God, the Spirit intercedes for us. To *intercede* means: *to stand between and make up the difference.* Abraham interceded as he stood between Lot and the judgment of God, and successfully pled his case. The Spirit stands between our limited understanding, and the full knowledge of God by giving us His utterances. They make up the difference, glory to God! If this were the only benefit of tongues it would be wonderful, but there are more.

*A person who speaks in tongues is **strengthened personally**, but one who speaks a word of prophecy strengthens the entire church. 1 Corinthians 14:4 (NLT)*

Speaking in tongues certainly can affect the world around you, but it also will set things in order *in* you. The Amplified Bible says he "edifies and improves himself." If you're interested in a self-help program, there's none better than the daily discipline of speaking in other tongues. Jude, the brother of the Lord, evidently saw the results of praying in tongues in his own life, and encouraged the rest of us to follow his practice.

But you, beloved, build yourselves up [founded] on your most holy faith [make progress, rise like an edifice higher and higher], praying in the Holy Spirit. Jude 1:20 (AMP)

I am interested in progressing through the different stages of my race in life. I do not want to find myself stuck in a holding pattern, not able to find my way to the next thing God has for me. The only way to make this kind of steady progress in the plan of God is to spend much time praying in the Spirit. This is one of the spiritual disciplines that we see in the lives of people who are greatly used of God.

Praying at all times in the Spirit, with all prayer and supplication. To that end keep alert with all perseverance, making supplication for all the saints. Ephesians 6:18

Praying at all times isn't the practice of most believers. Many have rejected this great blessing, and others, who have received the baptism in the Spirit, never take advantage of their ability to speak *God-talk*. Some would think their busy schedule prevents them from *praying at all times*, but prayer, praise, worship, and thanksgiving aren't just for special times. God-talk can flow wherever and whenever we have the opportunity: in our car, when there's downtime at work, when we are cleaning the house, etc.

And they were all filled with the Holy Spirit and began to speak in other tongues as the Spirit gave them utterance. Acts 2:4

The disciples began speaking in other tongues on the day of Pentecost. In diligently searching the New Testament, I have never been able to find where they stopped speaking. The flow continued throughout their lives. Let's follow their example and make God-talk our lifestyle.

Confession:

I will speak the utterances of the Spirit. My life progresses higher and higher as I speak in other tongues. I am praying effectively when I pray in tongues.

FULLNESS & BOLDNESS

*You prepare a table before me in the presence of my enemies; you anoint my head with oil; **my cup overflows**. Psalm 23:5*

Where do we normally find cups in use? At the dinner table. As we bring the cup of our hearts to His table of blessing, He fills us up to overflowing. Every part of our lives should reflect His fullness. However, God's definition of full is different than man's. He calls something full only when it's spilling out the top and running down the leg of the table, onto the floor. His fullness will cause a flood.

*[That you may really come] to know [practically, through experience for yourselves] the love of Christ, which far surpasses mere knowledge [without experience]; that you may be filled [through all your being] unto all the fullness of God [may have the richest measure of the divine Presence, and become a body **wholly filled and flooded with God Himself**]! Ephesians 3:19 (AMP)*

Spiritual fullness must be our main pursuit. If we want full satisfaction in other areas, such as our physical body or finances, we must first be full of God inside.

*Beloved, I pray that in all respects you may prosper and be in good health, **just as your soul prospers**. 3 John 1:2 (NASB)*

We will see prosperity all around us, if we'll learn to prosper inwardly. Some have learned to fill their lives with God's Word, but we also must become saturated with His Spirit. The disciples spent three years becoming full of the Word. They were living with The Living Word. But the Lord deemed that alone to be insufficient. We have seen that in Acts chapter 2, the disciples also were filled to overflowing with the Holy Spirit.

But others mocking said, "They are filled with new wine." Acts 2:13

They were so full that unknowledgeable people thought they were drunk from alcohol. No, the Holy Spirit had just filled their spirits to a level that overflowed. That spillover altered their physical senses, just as too much wine would, but with no negative after-effects. Peter gave the crowd a scriptural justification for this behavior:

*For these people are not drunk, as you suppose, since it is only the third hour of the day. But this is what was uttered through the prophet Joel: 'And in the last days it shall be, God declares, that **I will pour out my Spirit on all flesh**, and your sons and your daughters shall prophesy, and your young men shall see visions, and your old men shall dream dreams.' Acts 2:15-17*

Joel's prophecy was coming to pass then, in the beginning of the last days, and it is still being fulfilled today, toward the end of the last days, as God continues to pour out His Spirit. Paul stressed how important it is that every believer today not just become full, but learn to stay full.

*Don't be drunk with wine, because that will ruin your life. Instead, **be filled with the Holy Spirit**, singing psalms and hymns and spiritual songs among yourselves, and making music to the Lord in your hearts. Ephesians 5:18-19 (NLT)*

When the scripture says *be filled*, the language in the Greek denotes a continual action. It could literally read, *be constantly being filled*. The Amplified Bible says, "ever be filled." That means we never should allow ourselves to become dry and empty. We must live full, and stay full. In Acts 2, we saw the disciples filled to the point of spiritual drunkenness, and only two chapters later we see them getting filled again. That shouldn't surprise us. Any drunk will tell you that last week's binge isn't keeping him full this week!

*And when they had prayed, the place in which they were gathered together was shaken, and they **were all filled with the Holy Spirit and continued to speak the word of God with boldness**. Acts 4:31*

Notice that when they were full they were also bold. Boldness means that one is free from reservations and inhibitions; able to do and say anything that God wants them to do and say. Boldness is necessary in spreading the gospel. Paul desired greater boldness to speak, and he asked the churches to pray accordingly.

*And [pray] also for me, that [freedom of] utterance may be given me, that I may open my mouth to **proclaim boldly** the mystery of the good news (the Gospel). Ephesians 6:19 (AMP)*

A constant flow of the word and prayer combine to bring believers to a place of fullness and boldness. Peter came out of a prayer meeting in the upper room, was filled to overflowing, and displayed great boldness. When the great martyr Stephen was threatened with death, he boldly opened his mouth to speak for God. How did he become so bold? He lived full.

*But he, **full of the Holy Spirit**, gazed into heaven and saw the glory of God, and Jesus standing at the right hand of God. Acts 7:55*

In Acts 4:8, Peter is said to have been full of the Spirit. Now notice the 13th verse:

*Now **when they saw the boldness** of Peter and John, and perceived that they were uneducated, common men, they were astonished. And they recognized that they had been with Jesus. Acts 4:13*

It's not natural intelligence or education that are necessary to be great for God. Just get full, stay full, be bold, and watch great things happen!

Confession:

> *I'm living full of the Word. I'm living full of the Spirit, He fills me to overflowing as I drink long at His table. Rivers of living water flow out from me, and I am bold to do all that He tells me to.*

KNOWINGS AND LEADINGS

*But when he, the Spirit of truth, comes, he will guide you into all the truth. He will not speak on his own; he will speak only what he hears, and **he will tell you what is yet to come**. John 16:13 (NIV)*

Christians do not need to be unaware of what God wants for their lives. Great provision has been made for us to know what we need to know. Yes, we always will be required to live by faith, but faith makes movement, and we often need to know what steps to take in order to proceed in our faith-walk. God has given us His Spirit to bring us this kind of knowledge. He guides us into all truth and leads us through life.

For all who are led by the Spirit of God are sons of God. Romans 8:14

The Spirit's abiding presence is the birthright of every son of God (every believer). Why is He in us? Is He just an idle hitchhiker? No, He's in us to help us, and some of His most precious help comes as He shows us what we need to know.

My sheep hear my voice, and I know them, and they follow me. John 10:27

Following God completely requires hearing from Him accurately. How do we hear, or discern, the voice of God? We must first understand that God is a spirit, and He speaks to us *in our spirits*, through the person of the Holy Spirit. We must not look for, nor require, external leadings. Although God can, and sometimes does, speak to us through outward situations or other people, the bulk of His leadings happen inside us, where He is living.

*But the anointing that you received from him abides **in you**, and you have no need that anyone should teach you. But as his anointing teaches you about everything, and is true, and is no lie—just as it has taught you, abide in him. 1 John 2:27*

Our help is on the inside of us; that is where we must look. The anointing within will cast a vote of agreement when we hear truth. The more we learn to look to Him who is on the inside of us, the less frequently we will require the counsel of other people. Of course this does not diminish the role of teachers and leaders in the body, for it was God who placed them there for our benefit. The point is, we will know much in life by simply looking to the anointing within. We have *inside information*.

But you have been anointed by the Holy One, and you all have knowledge. 1 John 2:20

All we need to know is inside us. We know by the anointing, by the Spirit. Many people make the mistake of trying to hear an audible voice, expecting to hear a paragraph's worth of detail from God. That is not the primary way He leads. Normally, we will have a sense or impression that we are to go a certain way. Those kinds of leadings may seem unspectacular, but they are supernatural and have steered me to success many times. This ministry of the Spirit toward us began in our lives the moment we were born again, and He continues to lead us daily by the same inner witness.

The Spirit himself bears witness with our spirit that we are children of God. Romans 8:16

How do you know which way to go? See which direction seems best on the inside. Which option keeps rising up from within? As you consider all possible directions, check for the peace of God. One direction will seem best. That choice that brings more peace to you than any other is your answer, and it is a supernatural way of being led.

*Notwithstanding **it pleased Silas** to abide there still. Acts 15:34 (KJV)*

Silas had finished the assignment the apostles had given him in Antioch, and his partners in ministry left to go home. But something told Silas to stay around for another few days. It just so happened that, during that time, Barnabas split off from Paul, and Silas was invited to join Paul on his second missionary journey – a history-making event. These small leadings can affect major change in our lives.

But, as it is written, "What no eye has seen, nor ear heard, nor the heart of man imagined, what God has prepared for those who love him" these things God has revealed to us through the Spirit. For the Spirit searches everything, even the depths of God. 1 Corinthians 2:9-10

Knowledge that we need from God does not flow to us through our natural senses, it comes to us by His Spirit. The more we know Him, the more sensitive we will be to Him when He speaks to us. We know the main way He speaks to us is through His Word, but in the situations in life where we must receive specific direction, the Spirit stands ready to lead.

Now we have received not the spirit of the world, but the Spirit who is from God, that we might understand the things freely given us by God. 1 Corinthians 2:12

The precious things of God are mysterious and hidden from the world, but God desires to reveal His secrets to His church. We should be *in the know* concerning His plan for our lives, His plan for the earth, and things in the lives of our loved ones. At times, God will also allow us to supernaturally know things in order to help other people, some of whom we may never have met before.

To each is given the manifestation of the Spirit for the common good. For to one is given through the Spirit the utterance of wisdom, and to another the utterance of knowledge according to the same Spirit. 1 Corinthians 12:7-8

These spiritual gifts bring blessing to people's lives, direction is received, and Jesus is exalted and glorified. We must all understand that we can no longer get by just operating out of our heads. It's time to know and it's time to be led!

Confession:

> *I am His sheep and I hear His voice. He leads me and guides me in the way I should go. I know by the Spirit; I know by the anointing. I follow His peace. I never override the leading of the Spirit. He shows me things to come.*

ARE YOU A NEW CREATION?

The most important decision one can make in life is the decision to receive Jesus Christ as personal Lord and Savior. It is a decision to turn from sin and self, and follow God – every day and in every way.

This decision to receive Christ is what the Bible calls being born again, or being saved. Without this salvation experience, people are doomed to failure in life and eternity in hell. Success and eternal life belong to the believer in Christ. If you have been reading this book and do not know that you have been born again, it is time to make the decision to follow Christ.

Read what God says in His word about this great experience.

Truly, truly, I say to you, whoever hears my word and believes him who sent me has eternal life. He does not come into judgment, but has passed from death to life. John 5:24

For God so loved the world, that he gave his only Son, that whoever believes in him should not perish but have eternal life. For God did not send his Son into the world to condemn the world, but in order that the world might be saved through him. John 3:16-17

For by grace you have been saved through faith. And this is not your own doing; it is the gift of God, not a result of works, so that no one may boast. Ephesians 2:8-9

If you confess with your mouth that Jesus is Lord and believe in your heart that God raised him from the dead, you will be saved. For with the heart one believes and is justified, and with the mouth one confesses and is saved. Romans 10:9-10

Because our sin has separated us from God, we need a savior, one who would take our place in eternal death and give to us eternal life. Jesus is that savior; the only one qualified to take our place.

And this is the testimony, that God gave us eternal life, and this life is in his Son. Whoever has the Son has life; whoever does not have the Son of God does not have life. 1 John 5:11-12

Receive Christ right now by praying a prayer such as this one. Speak the words from your heart, and God will hear and answer you.

"Dear God, I see that my sins have separated me from You and I repent of sin. Thank You that you loved me so much that You sent Jesus to suffer and die on my behalf, so that I could receive eternal life. I believe Jesus died for me and rose again, and I receive Him as my Savior right now. Jesus, You are my Lord and I'll live for You from this day on. Thank You, Father for saving me!"

If you prayed that and meant it, be assured that God has done exactly what you asked. You are now His child. You have been born into his family. This verse now describes you – the new creation:

Therefore, if anyone is in Christ, he is a new creation. The old has passed away; behold, the new has come. 2 Corinthians 5:17

There are some additional steps you should take now that you are a follower of Jesus Christ. The most important step is to find a good local church. There will be a pastor there who will minister to you and help you grow in the things of God. Make sure your church believes and teaches the Bible and allows the Holy Spirit to work freely. Your pastor can help teach you about other steps to get started in the Christian life, such as studying the word of God, being filled with the Holy Spirit, tithing, and serving in the local church.

Congratulations on making the best decision of your life, and keep reading *New Creation Meditations!*

ABOUT THE AUTHOR

Faith in God's Word, and continual reliance on the Holy Spirit have been the keys to success in the life and ministry of Rev. Joel Siegel. Raised and educated as a Jew, Joel Siegel, at age 18, had a life-transforming encounter with Christ that brought him true purpose and fulfillment.

Rev. Joel Siegel began preaching and teaching the Word of God soon after he was saved in 1986. He entered full-time ministry in 1990, serving for three years as the music director for the acclaimed gospel music group Truth. Truth's road schedule took Joel and his wife Amy worldwide to over 300 cities a year, ministering in churches and on college campuses.

From 1993 to 2000, Joel was the musical director for Rev. Kenneth E. Hagin's RHEMA Singers & Band. In addition to assisting Rev. Hagin in his crusade meetings, he produced eight music CD's for the ministry, including his first solo release, Trust & Obey.

From 2000 to 2011, Joel and Amy (herself a skilled pastor and worship leader), served as the founding pastors of Good News Family Church in Orchard Park, NY. During this time, they were frequently asked to host shows for the TCT Christian Television Network. Joel regularly hosted their popular Ask The Pastor program.

Rev. Joel Siegel spends his time ministering to congregations in the US and abroad, passionately endeavoring to fulfill his assignment to help lead this generation into the move of God that will usher in the return of Christ.

The Siegel's make their home in Colorado. Joel oversees Faith Church Colorado in the town of Castle Rock, where Amy is lead pastor.

For music recordings, audio teaching series, books, and other resources by Joel Siegel, please visit www.biggodmedia.com.

To invite Rev. Joel Siegel to minister at a church or event, please visit www.joelsiegel.org.